Choosing to Live, Waiting to Die
Understanding Depression and Finding Hope

Maria Burgess

Choosing to Live, Waiting to Die: Understanding Depression and Finding Hope
Copyright © 2022 by Maria Burgess All right reserved
Published 2022

This book is not intending as a guide to diagnose or treat mental health conditions. Please seek out qualified physicians and mental health professionals if those services are required.

No part of this book may be reproduced, scanned, or distributed in any printed or electronic form without written permission of the author, with the exception of brief quotations in articles or reviews.

ISBN: 979-8-9858624-9-2

For my son, Joshua.
You are forever in my heart,
and remembered always.

Contents

Foreword ii
Introduction iii
The day my life ended .... - 1 -
What is depression? .... - 10 -
Healthy mind, healthy life .... - 22 -
Unseen: challenges in treatment .... - 38 -
Stigma, a death sentence .... - 54 -
The role of community leaders .... - 64 -
The fallacy of suicide prevention .... - 74 -
Hope in recovery is the best medicine. .... - 89 -
How to support/communicate with those you love .... - 99 -
Joshua's journal .... - 112 -
The Afterward ; .... - 125 -
    References and Resources .... - 139 -
    Acknowledgments .... - 142 -

Foreword

I met the Burgess family through my twin boys who are the same age as Joshua. They saw him almost daily and enjoyed his sense of humor, shared activities, and were amazed by his talents and how willing he was to share them with others. We received a call on a Sunday morning learning about his death, and the confusion, pain, and heartache as they cried for their friend was difficult to comfort them through. It has continued to impact them in innumerable ways.

As a psychologist, mother, and someone who has had many family members live with significant mental health conditions, Choosing to Live, Waiting to Die impacted me deeply. Maria, who is a licensed therapist, and has spent years helping individuals in need of mental health, has a beautiful way of describing her own experiences while weaving in important educational information. Watching the Burgess family, it would be easy to assume they would be immune from something like this happening. They clearly loved one another, spoke about mental health issues openly and honestly, were very present and playful, and enjoyed the time they spent with one another. This places Maria in a unique position to answer some important questions. She addresses how and why depression and mental health concerns impact individuals, and the need for these issues to be destigmatized and addressed at a community level.

We are in a time in which the rates of depression, anxiety, and mental health issues are skyrocketing, especially in children and adolescents. This book provides important information to help individuals struggling with depression and their friends, families, and community members that want to support them. I found it to be beautifully written, while providing important knowledge and tools that will help us to be more empathetic toward those we love. It is also a heartful tribute to Joshua from his loving mother.

Lorena Bradley, Ph,D, Licensed Clinical Psychologist

Introduction

On November 21, 2020, my life would be permanently altered by tragedy and loss. My 16-year-old son died suddenly from suicide. As my family and I grappled with the shock and the pain of this event, we had more questions than answers.

One of the worst things I have ever seen was the look on my nine-year old daughter's face when she asked, "why?". In the middle of my most painful moment, I needed to be able to say something to help my daughter in her worst moment. I told her the only things I knew. I told her, "I don't know. It doesn't make sense. We cannot make sense of things that are senseless. But I do know that your brother loved us, and he knew we loved him." Over the following days, I would hold onto that bit of knowledge and encourage my family to as well. That was and still is the most important answer.

Seeking answers after a tragic loss is important to healing. Without answers, our minds will come up with false information. Our memories will play tricks on us, and make us believe things that aren't true.

A wise person said to me, "Everyone will make sense of it, and that sense will be different for everyone."

In this book, I share my sense that I have learned from a senseless thing. My experiences and thoughts may not be what each individual experiences, but I am certain that some of what is contained in this book will resonate with each person. In order to successfully combat the challenge of mental illness, we must face it as a society. This book isn't intended to be used to diagnose or replace treatment for mental health disorders, but to inform and bring awareness of depression, the challenges associated, and that hope is possible with the right tools.

It is my hope that my words, while they can't answer every question, will answer some of the most important ones, and that they will begin a discussion in your life, with your family, with yourself, and with others. I hope to inspire you to share your story with others, to shed feelings of shame or guilt, and to heal.

While this book is the story of my family's experience, it is largely also educational and meant to broaden the understanding and perspective about mental health. There are elements of religion in it, as an important part of my life includes a strong religious community, but it is not a religious or spiritual book, and it is not meant to be.

If you are struggling with depression, please be aware of the potential for triggers in this book. Take your time, talk with those close to you, and if you do have thoughts of suicide, please reach out to a suicide hotline, or go to the ER.

I also write to help in my own healing, and for my son, whose story deserves to be told. May you be bolder, and persevere in your own mental health and in helping those you love.

*1-800-273-8255 is the national hotline and is available 24/7. There is also an option online for chat.

The day my life ended

I can remember very distinct things from the day that my world shattered. Some events from that day are seared into my mind, and visit me in living conscious nightmares. There are blank spaces as well. Things I can't recall through the fog in my mind. I don't remember the exact words that the police officer said to me, but I do remember the quiver in his voice and that it wasn't from the cold. How do you tell a mother that her son is no longer living? And when she says "What?" in disbelief, so you tell her again. And then when she asks, "Are you sure it is my son?" you have to again, confirm to her that her world has ended. To be the person who is standing on that line between the world making sense with color in it, and with a few words, that world is gone. What a terrible responsibility and weight he must have felt.

I remember sitting and waiting on my front steps, with no information about what had happened. The police were unable to tell me anything, because they were "investigating" and he died outside of city limits, so they had to wait for the county sheriff's office to take over. In my mind it was inconceivable. I ran through the scenarios, and knew suicide was potentially what had happened, but I didn't know specifics. It was equally possible in my mind that someone hurt him, or he was hit by a car. Why else would he be gone? Before he had left the house, he said, "I am going for a quick walk with the dog." He said it in a way that made me believe he would be back soon. He never came back.

When the dog came back alone and was barking on the front porch. I thought maybe Joshua had somehow gotten separated from him, or maybe Joshua thought he had put the dog in the backyard and the dog had somehow gotten around the house. I started to look for Joshua, at first annoyed that he hadn't taken care of the dog. I looked everywhere in the yard and in the house more than once. It wouldn't be the first time he didn't hear me calling for him, and was unable to hear because he was listening to something on his phone. I called the parents of his friends to see if they had heard from him, and I drove through the neighborhood and walked a couple of miles in the common areas he might be in. I would later find out that I had walked past where he had died. Even though I had a light on my phone, it wasn't very bright, and I didn't think to look for him on the ground. When I finally called dispatch, the first question the lady on the other end of the line asked me was, "Do you think he would commit suicide?" I didn't even know how to answer. My training told me, sure, that is possible with anyone and especially with teenagers, but my heart and mind rejected the possibility. I just told her I didn't know why else he would be gone so long, unless he was in trouble. I think about that now. How many times does this happen with teenagers, that that was the first question that she asked me?

After the police officer delivered the heart-breaking news to me, I waited for over an hour, without any additional information that would make sense of something that my mind was not comprehending. My body, however, understood something. I cannot describe the very real physical pain I was in, without any visible wounds. A friend came at that time and sat on the porch with me. Even though we didn't know each other well, he held me together as my heart broke, with his arm around my shoulder, and we waited. Waited to know what happened, and waited for my husband and my daughter to get home. I ignored my husband's calls because I could not tell him on the phone. I remember feeling that though he is worried for his son who had not come home when he should have, what a wonderful place to be. Wonderful that he still had the luxury to worry. I no longer worried. My son was beyond a place where my worry for him would help him anymore. The police office got permission to tell me that they were considering it to be a suicide, but officially they had to complete an investigation, and I received that information without my family with me.

I remember telling my husband and our daughter, Anna, who was my son's best friend when they finally arrived. I watched the sorrow on their faces as their worlds ended as well. Afterwards, we sat the other two younger girls down and told them. I think I was the one to tell them, but I can't remember that part. But I don't know if I will ever forget the absolute devastation on the face my nine-year-old, Sarah, when she asked "why?". I have never seen that kind of pain on any of my children's faces. And I remember the impression in my mind that a part of them had died as well. I didn't only lose my son that night. I lost myself, I lost my husband, and my children. In just a moment, their childhood was destroyed. Their sense of safety was gone in an instant.

It may seem hard to understand when I say we died that day, but that doesn't make it any less true. The people we were before are gone, along with my son. Often times, when a person experiences a true tragedy or trauma, they will talk about "before" and "after", because everything is marked by that. You can't unknow the things that you have learned since the tragedy. You see the world differently, and it paints every interaction you have had or will have. It changes you on a cellular level.

A critical aspect of a tragedy, is the unexpectedness of it. One minute the world is one way, and now it isn't. One minute you are safe, and your loved ones are safe, and now you don't think safety is even a real thing. And it makes you question if it ever existed.

That day started out like any normal Saturday. I woke up a little early for a Saturday, to take my son to a driver's education class. Being my oldest, and being new to driving, I was constantly worried that he would have a moment where he wasn't paying attention, or his inexperience would lead to an accident. Over the last few months, I had him practice. And then realizing there were limits to my husband's and my ability to teach, we signed him up for a class that met every Saturday for three weeks. So, I had him drive across town that morning with me sitting in the passenger seat. He got irritated at me, as teenagers do, because I kept telling him when the traffic lights changed to yellow or red. I am sure he said something along the lines of "I can see it, Mom.". I told him, "Joshua, you once stopped in the middle of an intersection because you didn't judge the light right. You have gotten a lot better, but I am a little jumpy. The more you drive well, the less jumpy I will be. It is your job to be consistent enough that I forget the need to tell you. If I didn't trust you driving at this point, you wouldn't be driving today. I am trusting you with my life, my new car, and my baby in the car". The "baby" being him. He didn't really respond to that, and we got to the school with little trouble. How I miss the worry, and the stress of teaching him the things he needs to know. Or irritating him with my parenting. As with most teenagers, they love that their parents are there teaching them and involved, but are also irritated, because they are trying to grow independent from them. Teenagers need to do that in order to build confidence in their own abilities.

That day was so ordinary. Maybe that is part of why it is such a shock for that to have been the day. There wasn't anything remarkable about it. I spent the day grocery shopping and doing Saturday chores, and spending time with the younger two girls. I also spent a bit of time relaxing because it had been such a long week. I was a "single mom" that week as my husband was on a hunting trip with our oldest daughter. We had gone back and forth about whether Joshua should have gone too, but he had been stressed about school, and really didn't seem that interested. So, he went to his classes.

When I picked him up from driver's ed, we talked about normal things. He told me how he felt that class that day covered examples of situations that were uncommon, and so he felt it didn't apply as much. My husband called on Facetime while we were driving home, but we couldn't hear him. I think he was trying to show us the wild turkeys where he was, but was trying to stay quiet. I know it bothers my husband that he didn't get to talk to Joshua that day. He hadn't seen him that whole week. You see, we sent Anna, with him, because she had been struggling with her own challenges and felt it would be best for her to have a break from her regular things and spend some one-on-one time with her dad. Research shows that those connections with adults are a protective thing for youth. It restores those bonds they have in their early years and can help them through the teenage transition phase. He was also just excited to spend time with his daughter on her first hunting trip which had become a tradition and sort of a rite of passage.

My husband and I talked about our kids regularly, and tried to figure out what were the best things at each stage for each of them. We knew that you get some things wrong as parents, but the connections you make, can make so many other things insignificant.

On the ride home, Joshua asked me if we had any plans that night, which is a normal question for the kids to ask when they want to make their own plans. When I asked him "why?", at first, he said something along the lines of "no reason, just curious," and then he said that a couple of his friends, had planned to go on a double date with him, and he just needed to find a date. When I asked him more details, like "when are you going?", "How late is the place open?", "Who are you going with?", he seemed frustrated that he didn't have answers to my questions, and he locked up.

Before that we had discussed that his dad and sister would be back the next day. I remember him saying "They will be back tomorrow?" but the tone he used was peculiar, though I didn't know why, and I dismissed it as another teenage thing that I couldn't interpret. But the tone was peculiar and he didn't seem excited that they would be back. After that day, I would recall that conversation, and think maybe he believed he was out of time. You see, he had access to his chosen method of suicide and knew that he didn't normally have that access. Maybe he believed it would be harder to follow through with his plan if Anna was home, or his dad, because more people would be there. He had also had a week to be disconnected from them. This is all speculation. We can never completely know what was going on in those moments before a person dies from suicide.

When we were talking about his plans for the night, I sensed that my questioning was further aggravating him, and expressed my frustration with his lack of ability to participate in the conversation. I stepped out of the vehicle to run into Walgreens to pick up some prescriptions, took a moment to cool down, and came back. I told him I was sorry for my frustration with the situation, but I knew he had been having a hard time lately, and I wanted to make sure things happened that night, knowing that getting out with friends would do him good. I told him "I feel that if I don't help you make this happen, I am afraid you will be depressed, and it will be my fault for not helping."

I remember his body visibly deflating, and he sighed like he was tired and said, "You don't have to do that mom.". That conversation would haunt me for months afterwards. It was the first time I had used that word. Depressed. What does that even mean?

I remember being completely shocked, like a rug had been pulled out from under me when he died, but I look back and remember that conversation. I remember a couple of times over the last couple of months where he seemed to be having a hard time. But they were so few, and they didn't last. Every time, he appeared to be struggling, we talked to him. We checked in with him. And he would say just enough for us to think, he will be ok, even if he isn't happy about some things.

He bought brownies for his sisters during one of the breaks in his class that day. He left them for his sisters. When I bought cookies later, he said "I see how it is. Trying to show me up". He was teasing of course, but it still hurts looking back. When we got home, I dished out dinner. Kentucky Fried chicken, you know, because it had been a long day and I was tired. I put aside the biggest piece for him, as I usually did, because he was always hungry as teenage boys can be. He also liked to weight lift, so he was always watching his protein intake.

He told me he wasn't that hungry, or maybe he didn't feel like eating. That got me turning my head. I am sure I asked him what was going on. Did he feel sick? Did he have a big lunch or eat something that has left his stomach unsettled? It doesn't seem to matter how old your child is, a mom is very aware of what her kids are eating. I can't even guess how many times I've lectured the children about eating all of their food groups, and drinking enough water. Joshua responded with, "I think I can make it work." I remember telling him I didn't want him to eat a big meal if he wasn't feeling well, and he dismissed it. He ate his chicken. That was the one and only time I can recall that his appetite had changed. He joked, "Anna is going to be so mad when she finds out we had KFC!" knowing it was her favorite fast food and we don't get it often.

So, you see, there were signs, but they were buried by normalcy. And knowing that does not bring peace to a sad and broken heart.

From the day a baby is born, a mother develops an anxiety. I think it is biologically wired into a mother to ensure her offspring make it to adulthood. In every situation, we, as mothers determine the biggest risk factors for our children. We assume that the worst scenario is serious injury or death, and then we remove the danger if we can. When we take our children to the park, we scan for suspicious strangers. We analyze whether traffic close to the park is dangerous, and look for dangers on the equipment. And then we factor in the personality of our child. Is my child a daredevil, and will she climb on the equipment in a way it wasn't intended? You know you can't keep your child completely safe from everything, but you remove the biggest threats, and you talk to your child. You educate them and hope they will hear you, knowing that they aren't even aware of some of the dangers because their world experience is so limited. But you can't keep them locked up, because that is also not good for them. So, you do your best to make life safe, and you swallow your fears. You dismiss the anxieties that seem over the top in an effort to give your child life experiences.

As our children have gotten older, I remember telling my husband that even though they are smart and gifted, their brains have not fully developed so their ability to problem solve is impaired. We also have less and less control every year. I told him that we just have to pray that they make it through adolescence and that the stupid choices they make aren't too bad, just like we did at that stage.

When looking back, we can see how COVID really made Joshua feel isolated. It is so difficult for my husband and I to see people wear masks, especially the youth. For youth like my son, who felt that if he disappeared, his friends would not care, and that no one would really be impacted. How hard is it to realize differently, when you are in a room full of people and you never see them smile? In our culture, a smile is the accepted signal that your presence makes someone happy.

The night after he died, our Bishop, and our Stake president were in our home. A Bishop and Stake President are religious leaders for our local community in our practiced religion. Joshua was friends with the bishop's son and the Stake President's daughter, who was also one of the friends he was supposed to be with that night. They came to offer support to us. I remember little about it, but it was essential at that time. All of the support we received was essential.

I remember peeking out the window after they had left, and the bishop's body was visibly caving in. The Stake president put his arm around him. The bishop had a pretty significant relationship with Joshua. He was part of our village; helping us raise our child, and had met with Joshua many times. He blamed himself. I think most people blamed themselves after his passing. How could they not see? Why did this happen? If only we had known. If only we had called him, or had come to the house that night. If only we had invited him over more. If only we had talked more with him. If only. If only. If only. These thoughts would spin circles for me, my family, and all those who loved him.

You ever get in a fender bender, and think, "if I had reacted quicker, maybe this would not have happened." Like somehow, we can have control of our world if we are just more vigilant. If we are stronger. If we hadn't been tired. If we had been smarter. More loving. Just more. And because we weren't someone else paid the price, and there is no bringing them back.

As the weeks and months passed, I would fight that. And I know others would as well. His friends all struggled with his passing. A couple of them were more vulnerable themselves, and had been hospitalized in the months after. I had parents who knew Joshua approach me expressing fear for their own children. They knew that if someone like Joshua, who presented well, and didn't show the typical signs, could die, it could be any of their children as well. A youth leader from our church, expressed to me after that she felt all of the kids should be on suicide watch, because based off of him, they were all in danger.

We would seek to find understanding when there wasn't enough information to make sense out of this tragedy. But in this book, I hope to create more understanding for others about what depression looks like and feels like, and why it is hard to explain for those who are experiencing it. I hope to give words to those living with depression so they can reach out, to assist loved ones in understanding a little more what is happening to someone struggling with depression and to create clarity about what things they have control of and what they don't. The sad reality is that we are all affected by depression. Every single person has someone in their circle who is struggling silently with depression.

Statistics on depression and suicide are easy to find. The CDC reports that suicide is the 10th leading cause of death in the US in all age groups (CDC). Every day 130 Americans die by suicide, which is one every 11 minutes. Depression affects 20-25% of Americans 18+ in a given year. 48, 000 Americans die by suicide every year. Only half of Americans experiencing a diagnosis of major depression receive treatment (NAMI). Eighty to ninety percent of people who seek treatment for depression are treated successfully using therapy and/or medication (TADS study). Suicide is the 2nd leading cause of death in both the US and the world for those aged 15-24 years (CDC). Suicide and accidental death compete for the number one cause of death among youth.

When we interpret those statistics, it is glaringly obvious that this is a very dangerous disease. It is also important to recognize that there are different degrees of lost life. Somebody may still be breathing but is not able to live their life. The people who are surviving depression are also missing out on opportunities in their work or education. Their relationships are impacted. Their ability to enjoy their lives and be productive is greatly impacted and we all miss out on what they have to offer.

For every death caused by this disease, there are dozens, if not hundreds of people negatively affected by that death, who may also experience depressive symptoms as a result. This is a far-reaching disease. So. why do we know so much and yet so little? Why are more people suffering and dying from this disease than before?

What is depression?

I remember listening to a TED talk once, by Andrew Solomon, where he shares his own experience with depression and comments made by others that he has interviewed. One person described depression as "a slower way of being dead". Andrew went on to explain that when you are depressed, you do not believe that you are looking through a fog or veil of depression, but that the veil of happiness has been lifted and you are now seeing how the world really is.

Imagine you could feel yourself dying. You do not have the energy to enjoy anything, and the amount of energy you do have is reserved for basic functions of life, such as breathing, staying awake, and eating just enough to not starve. When a person is near death, their appetite diminishes as their internal systems are shutting down and the same need for caloric intake isn't there. If you've never experienced that kind of feeling, then wonderful! But perhaps you know someone who has experienced this.

When a person is in a severe and chronic state of depression, this is how it can feel. It isn't something someone is choosing, but something that is happening with internal hormones and neurotransmitters, and it is a complex disorder. Neurotransmitters are chemicals in the brain that allow the brain to communicate by connecting neurons or nerve cells. Some of the neurotransmitters mostly associated with depression are dopamine, serotonin, norepinephrine, noradrenaline, oxytocin, and endorphins. We all have all of these and they operate in different ways to control everything from emotions, to basic bodily functions. Any disruption or a deficiency of these will cause unwelcome symptoms.

Dopamine is the chemical that communicates with the front of the brain, and stirs the emotions of pleasure or reward. It can also increase concentration and awareness. Serotonin can affect body temperature, hunger, and sleep. This neurotransmitter builds up the desire to have feelings of appetite, arousal, and a positive mood. Noradrenaline produces the "fight or flight" response, and Norepinephrine works in conjunction with noradrenaline to calm the body when the danger has passed. Oxytocin is the chemical that creates the emotions that allow us to be social, and is associated with emotions such as empathy, connectedness, and feeling close. Endorphins are associated with elevated moods, and can produce that feeling runners or other athletes get that allow them to run that extra mile, or a "runner's high." This is a simplification of neurochemistry but the takeaway is that these things affect mood and cognitive abilities.

I want to be clear that I will be describing multiple examples of how depression is experienced, as it presents in various ways. Someone may have all of the symptoms of depression every time they have an episode, or they may only have some of the symptoms of depression in different episodes because the catalyst or cause is different.

If you are reading this book, you probably have concerns for someone in your life, want to understand others, or you, yourself are experiencing symptoms of depression. That is an advantage that not many have. Take a moment to acknowledge that advantage, even though it doesn't feel like one. Especially, when you are experiencing depressive symptoms, or it's been a while since you've seen your loved one happy. There is an advantage to being in a position of awareness. Knowledge is power. It will sound completely bonkers, but I have had thoughts of envy when I have heard others' stories of those who have had loved ones act out of character before dying from suicide. Or maybe their loved one is still fighting chronic depression and experiencing suicidal ideation. What a terrible thing to be envious of! But I envy that they had a chance to act, and a chance to seek treatment. Think of it like cancer. Maybe a loved one is screened earlier and able to get treatment. Maybe they survive and go into remission, or they fight for months or years and don't survive the cancer later. All sickness is awful, but having a chance to fight, knowing they were sick is something. But in the end, getting to hold them a little longer and maybe give them support while they were dying. (I do recognize that strange thoughts and feelings occur with complicated grief and I am not minimizing the grief of others and their losses.)

When a person dies suddenly there is no support for them as they die. Joshua had been dying for a while, and we just didn't know it. Do you think I would have gotten on him about his grades If I had known, or do you think I would have held him a little longer when I would hug him? It might not have changed anything, but it would have been nice to have had the option.

In the days after his death, there were some things that have stuck with me. My youngest, who was nine at the time, said "It is a nightmare.", and his other sister said, "I wished it had been a car accident.". Can you imagine a world where you wished a loved one had died from an accident? Obviously, you wish your loved one to be with you most of all, and you don't want anything bad to happen to them, but we accept to some degree that accidents do happen and are sometimes unavoidable. A person who loses someone in a car accident will still struggle with those thoughts of wondering if things could have happened differently to change things, but with suicide it feels like it is completely avoidable and therefore it has to be someone's fault. They may place blame on the person who died, the family, friends, or a number of other things. This is an inaccurate way to view suicide. Events and people influence suicide, but there is not a causality between these things.

I had so many loving people say to me after, "I can only imagine.". That is the truth of it. I appreciated those words. Much more helpful than someone saying, "I understand how you feel." No person can really completely understand another's experience. But going through something like this does bond you with others who have lost someone this way. Those weird thoughts that you have, don't seem so crazy to someone who has also experienced it. You can't explain it.

Just as hard as it is for us to explain our story to someone, because you can't really know without living it, someone who experiences depression has limited ability to describe it to another who has not. But if we can respond with "I can only imagine" in a validating way, we can clear the path to where we don't have to understand to be understanding. We can be by their side in a way we couldn't otherwise.

My first experience with depression was after having my first child. I can look back on it and identify that it was from sleep deprivation brought on by medical conditions that prevented restful sleep. There is a link between sleep, cognitive function, and mood. The episode that I experienced was a mild case of depression, but still very painful. I didn't even call it depression. I really just thought I was being "emotional", but at the time I remember telling my husband that it felt like a dark cloud was always there, and I would just get weepy all of the time, and I hated that. I was not a "crier". I was a strong, intellectual woman, dang it! And I believed, mistakenly, that tears were a sign of weakness. You know the feeling when it has been overcast for several days or maybe weeks, and you just feel off. It's difficult to describe that feeling. We don't really have a good word for it.

My first major episode of depression was also postpartum, but this time it was after my second child. Again, due to lack of sleep related to medical conditions. I had not slept for more than 30-45 minutes at a time for months. I was a young mom, 22 years old, and still did not identify it as depression, because that is not how I would have described it. I would have described it as intense fatigue. And I hated that I couldn't shake that off. I felt like a bad mother. If I couldn't be a good mother, what was my worth? I only started getting suspicious that things were off when I started to try to figure out why I felt unhappy. I had a loving and supportive husband, and two beautiful and healthy children. I didn't have anything serious going wrong in my life. If I had, maybe I would never have known something was wrong because I would have blamed it on that. But I felt ashamed. Why couldn't I just have more gratitude? Why couldn't I be a little less lazy? Maybe if I exercised more? I did confide in my husband that I was struggling, and that I felt bad that I was struggling. Thank goodness, he didn't judge me for that. He just stood by me and asked how he could help.

It wasn't until months after my symptoms were alleviated that I finally told my husband that I had had thoughts that I was better off never waking up. It wasn't a desire to die. It was a feeling of being too exhausted to live. I didn't tell him while I was experiencing these thoughts, because he was a supportive loving husband who felt part of his purpose in life was to make me happy. I thought he would blame himself, and I wanted to protect him from that. I believe Joshua also felt this way and in his struggle was trying to protect those he cared about, not knowing that this was the thing that would hurt them the most.

Along with fatigue, feelings of worthlessness, and passive suicidal ideation, I also experienced brain fog. That last one is hard to identify in yourself. How can you identify fog when you are in it? But it makes recall difficult and problem solving in normal, everyday challenges incredibly difficult or impossible. It looks like someone asking you a normal question, and you find yourself incapable to answer. Then you feel uncomfortable because the answer is simple, but you're just incapable of producing it. It is incredibly frustrating. From the outside that looks like someone looking confused more than normal, but again it takes a while for that pattern to be noticeable. For someone experiencing it, they will not see it as a symptom or as something happening to them. They will start to feel dumb or incapable. They will make silly mistakes, and rather than being able to identify that something is happening to them, they will suppose it to be something wrong with themselves. They will likely blame themselves and then they will attach a negative self-worth to that.

I remember when my step-grandmother started to have issues with her memory late in her life. It was hard to identify because she would sometimes appear confident in her memories. It took my mother talking to her other siblings to see if they too were noticing something off. Grandma had very little awareness of her memory loss, and cognitive decline. It wasn't until it was severe, that those around her were certain that there was something going on beyond the occasional forgetfulness that we all experience from time to time. So, when a loved one is repeatedly saying stuff like, "I got nothing out of school today, "or work, or whatever, it is important to take note of that. They may seem like they are just tired or it was just an off day, but this is something to watch for and look for patterns. Try not to dismiss it as maybe they are daydreaming or thinking about other stuff, especially if it is not a normal thing for them.

Several things can be a catalyst for a depressive episode. It is important to not just think about depression as a state of mind. It is a disease, but it is also a symptom of other diseases. That last bit is important. We often simplify depression in our mind as maybe a person had some difficult thing in their life and they never bounced back. While environmental factors do affect depression, they aren't the cause of it. If those factors were the cause, then anyone who has a good life would never be depressed, and we know that simply isn't true. It also means that anyone who has bad things happen in their life would be depressed, and this is also not true, though it is reasonable to assume that someone going through difficult things is more likely to experience depression. Why is that, besides for the obvious reason?

There has been loads of research done on how trauma affects the brain and body. Basically, the findings are that when a person has experienced an adverse event, their body will store that stress. It alters how the brain operates and affects every system in the human body. Think about it in this way; if a person is repeatedly hurt, physically or mentally, the brain receives multiple hits of adrenaline and cortisol which can cause a physiological reaction and change in neurological activity. Maybe it makes it difficult to concentrate, so you start to do poorly in school or work, or you start acting more irritable in your relationships, so you start losing your support systems. Now the message you are starting to get is that you aren't good at things. You aren't capable. You can't keep a job. You hurt the people in your life. You start to believe that you have little worth, and that people are better off without you. You are learning these things with repeated negative feedback in your environment. Leading you to believe it's because you are screwing up. It isn't your fault, as something internal is happening to you. Brain fog makes it difficult to recognize what is happening and that this is not a reflection of your strength or character, but something else.

We learn things through repetition, causing neural pathways to be established in our brains. Think of the brain as wild bush country without any roads. With new life experiences, you start creating pathways, and at first it is hard to find those pathways because they aren't well traveled. As you travel them more often, the pathways are easier to find, and traverse. This is similar to when you move to a new neighborhood. It takes longer to find things at first, but after time, it becomes almost automatic. Our experiences in life make these pathways, and how we interpret these experiences also matters. Elevated emotions associated with experiences affect those pathways as they will be the easiest to access or recall. Kind of like a landmark. A memory associated with a high amount of fear such as a near drowning will be a much bigger or easily found pathway, especially if near water. The same thing happens with every emotion. A particularly happy memory of a family vacation will be easy to recall. If you think back to your earliest memories as a child, the ones that you are able to bring to the surface are events with high emotion. Memories with neutral emotions are more difficult to recall.

Take two individuals, both have just lost their job, which is usually considered a stressful life event. While both individuals will associate the situation with negative emotion, their thoughts about the event will be different. Maybe one has had people in their life tell them that they will never accomplish anything, so they are more likely to see that employment loss as more evidence that they are a failure. Maybe the other individual was taught that they can learn from their experiences. So, they interpret the situation as there is something better ahead of them. And these aren't always intentionally taught things. Sometimes it is how they have seen others approach situations or speak about those types of life events.

So, one pathway is how they think about the event, and that will also be connected to an emotion. Other connecting pathways are thoughts about what to do with those thoughts, or emotions, and how to cope with the situation. Most of us are not 100% aware of this process and will find ourselves acting on a feeling without understanding where that feeling originated. This can vary in produced outcomes or consequences. Maybe they have learned that using alcohol makes it better. Perhaps they have learned to reach out for support from loved ones. Whatever that may be is very individualized, and also will change throughout their life. Everyone will have different connecting routes based on an accumulation of life experiences, but all will have helpful and unhelpful routes. There isn't a single person who only has helpful, or unhelpful routes.

Now the ability to choose which connection is made, is determined by various things. Sometimes it isn't really a conscious decision so much as stumbling on to the most well-traveled route. Maybe it is clear what the best path to take is. But suppose there is fog. Or maybe it is dark, and now you are trying to find those (mental) pathways in the dark. And you've got other cross-sections or interference as well. Like the electricity bill is due, and you have to take care of that. Or an assignment in school. Or you have to address the needs of your children. And a million other things. So, decisions do not occur inside of a vacuum. And if we could just address one thing at a time, we would probably choose more correctly more often. But the more stressors we have occurring at the same time, the more difficult it is for the brain to stay on the most helpful pathways or connections. The brain has something like 100 billion neurons and generates 1500 new neural connections a day. Actually, I can't even say if those numbers are correct because every time more research is done on the brain, it seems that those numbers increase. Some research claims much higher numbers than those. The brain is amazing but it also doesn't take much for things to become disordered or disrupted, or for us to learn maladaptive thought patterns.

Let's go back to the fog, or low-light conditions. Researchers do not know all of the medical reasons why depression occurs, but there is enough information available to know that it always has some brain chemistry component. The Mayo Clinic has done some interesting research on neural activity in the brain. If you google Mayo clinic PET brain scan, you will see an image pop up comparing a non-depressed brain with a depressed brain. Brain activity shows up as white and yellow. In a brain without depression, the scan looks like Las Vegas at night. In the brain of an individual with a depressed brain, it looks like a power outage indicating decreased brain activity. There will be a website listed in the reference section for convenience.

In a depressed brain, the connections are not happening as they should. This is the fog, or the low-light. This is what impairs your ability to see clear pathways. As the situation (depression) worsens, the harder it is for connections to be made that allow you to understand your emotional response to something and problem solve your way through it. You are only able to see the challenge, but you can't see your way out.

So, each episode of depression has both an environmental, and a brain chemistry component. It isn't only situational depression, and it isn't an imbalance of the brain alone; it is both. To figure out what the specific components of an episode are, requires evaluation from a professional, and usually a team of both medical and mental health experts to diagnose and treat. Depression is a complex disorder and requires more advanced assessment and outside help.

One of the diagnostic tools used in mental health assessments is the Patient Health Questionnaire, or PHQ-9, which was developed to not only diagnose depression but also assess the severity. It isn't a complete picture, but it is a good place to start. It is important to note that just because someone experiences depression, does not mean they will always have it. It goes back to that idea of what the initial onset is. You may think it is because of the loss of a job, and maybe returning to employment will alleviate symptoms, but that is just the catalyst. The underlying learned pathways are still there, and maybe the unhelpful ones will be dismissed, or the next time that person experiences a rejection or adverse event, those unhelpful pathways are still connected and more developed. This is why it gets complicated because these are all internal processes. Medical conditions, deficiencies in brain chemistry, abnormal hormone regulation, unhelpful/helpful coping skills, and stage of life, all affect a persons' mental health.

The PHQ-9 contains nine main questions. A person will mark each of those nine things as something they either have, or haven't experienced within the last two weeks. There is another distinction of how often that symptom is occurring. Is it occurring for several days, more than half of the days, or nearly every day? The more frequent that symptom is

WHAT IS DEPRESSION?

experienced, the higher the score, which ultimately determines the severity of the depression. The list of symptoms includes:
1. Little interest or pleasure in doing things.
2. Feeling down, depressed, or hopeless.
3. Trouble falling or staying asleep.
4. Feeling tired or having little energy.
5. Poor appetite or overeating.
6. Feeling bad about yourself-or that you are a failure or have let yourself or your family down.

7. Trouble concentrating or things such as reading the newspaper or watching TV.

8. Moving or speaking so slowly that other people could have noticed. Or the Opposite-being so fidgety or restless that you have been moving around a lot more than usual.

9. Thoughts that you would be better off dead, or of hurting yourself.

There is actually a tenth question that asks if any of these symptoms have made doing things in your life difficult. I don't know why this isn't included in the same way as the first nine, but my guess is that you can have someone experiencing symptoms that can still "function" in a semi-normal way. Behavior is not always indicative of depression.

According to the Diagnostic and Statistical Manual of Mental Disorders (DSM), a person has to experience multiple symptoms of depression for more than two weeks to be diagnosed with Major Depressive Disorder (MDD). The symptoms must also not be due to substance abuse or another medical condition. Someone can have a medical condition that leaves them bed ridden, or they have chronic pain, and they can have experienced all of these symptoms of depression due to that medical condition, but it will not be classified as MDD. The symptoms will still be treated the same way, and a doctor may prescribe medication to help, or therapy to help cope with the medical condition, but the distinction on a medical chart will read "depressive symptoms,", not Major Depressive Disorder. If the medical condition is treated and is resolved, but the depressive symptoms remain for a length of time, a MDD diagnosis may be appropriate.

Another tool that is used in assessing mental health is actually an acronym; FIDO, meaning frequency, intensity, duration, and onset. Each of these items is important to understanding whether a person is experiencing an episode of depression, or if it is a chronic condition. The onset of their condition gives some clue on how to treat it. Each case of depression needs to be treated individually. You can have a case where someone experiences mild symptoms of depression for 20 years, where it never progresses but makes them vulnerable. Another possibility is someone who has never experienced any depression and suddenly they are having thoughts of ending their life. Immediately the onset becomes important. Did a new medication create this symptom? It's possible that treatment in this case is a safety plan and stopping the medication causing the issue. You can also have a case where someone experiences severe and persistent Major Depressive Disorder. This person can be chronically ill and will struggle to maintain productivity in their lives. A multi-disciplinary approach is recommended in this case, with a treatment team to include a primary care physician, psychiatric care, and therapy. There are other options such as outpatient day rehabilitation programs to improve productivity and socialization. Just like when a person is diagnosed with cancer, there isn't a one size fits all treatment like in previous generations when we knew less about the illness. Every case was treated the same. Fortunately, we have more information than ever before.

One thing to bring attention to on the PHQ-9 are symptoms you may not think of as symptoms. Feelings of worthlessness is a symptom. We usually dismiss this as bad self-esteem, but it is actually a sign of depression. A poor self-esteem by itself does not qualify as depression, but if it is present with other symptoms, it can be. We often think of self-esteem as a conditional state. Some people have low self-esteem, right? Especially among teenagers. We need to start teaching them that a low self-esteem shouldn't be treated as normal, and is actually abnormal and an unhealthy state of mind. It is at the very least a vulnerability for depression to occur.

Because low self-esteem or feelings of worthlessness is a symptom, when we recognize its presence, we need to start looking to see if that person is experiencing other indicators of depression. Oftentimes, a person experiencing low self-worth, will not see it that way. They will have thoughts like, "I don't matter,", "I'm never going to make it on varsity,", "I am never going to get that raise,", "I can't finish college,", "I'm just not smart enough,", "My wife is unhappy with me, that means I am a failure,", or, "I am ugly.". These are thoughts, but thoughts can be problematic. A healthy mind can have these thoughts, but will be able to recognize that no one fails all of the time. It will be able to focus on learning from mistakes, and believe that their worth isn't measured by accomplishment, but by inherent value. But an unhealthy mind will become stuck.

The other symptom I want to talk about is suicidal ideation, in which there are different types as well as levels of severity. Suicidal ideation is on a spectrum just like every other symptom. At the low end, there is passive ideation or the feeling of "I don't want to wake up tomorrow, it's too hard". On the extreme end, there is active suicidal ideation which is when a person has a plan, a method, and an intention to carry it out. And then there are other points in between on that spectrum. It is important to understand that suicidal ideation is not a choice, just like the example above of feeling worthless. We all experience those thoughts from time to time, and we call that automatic thinking in the mental health world. These are thoughts that occur automatically, which a healthy mind will be able to dismiss as an errant thought.

With suicidal ideation, the illness is severe enough that thoughts of dying are occurring automatically, and the person has limited ability to dismiss them. And actually, at that point dismissing them is dangerous. A person experiencing suicidal thoughts will often be scared of those thoughts, because the part of the brain that still feels a natural fear of death is functioning. As a consequence of that fear, they will try to ignore them. They internally dismiss it like, "That's crazy. I'm not crazy.". The more those thoughts occur, the worse they will feel about themselves. They fear that they cannot control their mind. So, they hide it from themselves until the suicidal thoughts become constant in their everyday life. They are on one of those pathways mentioned earlier, and that pathway is in a fog so thick, that they cannot figure out which direction they came from, or how to get out.

The following two pictures were both taken by Joshua in 2020. The first one was on one of his runs. This was an area he enjoyed running regularly, and a place where we walked often as a family. The second one is taken in the same area moments before he died. It was heartbreaking for my husband and I to discover this last photo Joshua took and the very real illustration of the darkness that he was experiencing in his mind, especially when in contrast to how his mind was when healthiest.

WHAT IS DEPRESSION?

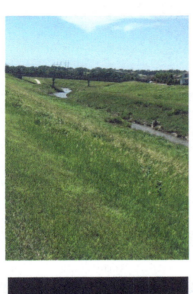

Healthy mind, healthy life

With depression, you don't experience life in full color. Food can become unappetizing, and the things you once enjoyed are no longer enjoyable or appealing. Let's compare this to the varying experiences people had with COVID during the outbreak in 2020. Some carried the disease but didn't really experience many, if any symptoms, while others were hospitalized, fighting for their lives. Some individuals were considered more vulnerable, because of age or preexisting conditions, such as diabetes, or other health conditions that affect breathing. These vulnerable individuals had varied outcomes, ranging from mild to severe or fatal. This is like depression. We cannot predict exactly who will get it, or who will fall from it. We simply don't know enough about it yet.

One of the most peculiar symptoms of COVID is the loss of taste or smell. Not everyone who had COVID experienced this, but those who did would probably describe it as disconcerting to now have one of their senses missing. Why do some only experience that for a few days, and others for weeks or longer after? This was more than just being stuffed up with congestion. This was an absence of that sense.

For a person who is going through depression, this is what life becomes like. They are going through the motions, and are experiencing life, but things are no longer interesting to them, or pleasurable. And it is not always detectable. There is not a clear idea of how long the symptoms will last if nothing is done to treat them. There is a great fear that they will never feel "normal" again.

I remember the June before my son passed away, I had a trip planned to go to the Great Smoky National Forest. He was not interested in going at all. I asked him what he would rather do, and he just said he didn't want to miss out on working out and hanging out with friends. At the time, everyone was staying away from social gatherings, so he was primarily connecting with friends through texting. I told him that there was a gym at the resort we were staying at, plus we had physical activities planned. But he did not care, and, I was so annoyed by his apathy. It came across as ungrateful, and my feelings were hurt. Every year I tried to plan special family trips and our scrap books are full of adventures. It seemed, at the time, that my son had finally reached the stage of teenagerhood where he no longer wanted to spend time with me. I had heard about it, but hadn't expected it, as we were pretty close.

In addition to the lack of interest in going on that trip, he mostly just followed along wherever we went without really engaging most of the time while there, but on that trip, I think his favorite activity was tubing down a river in Tennessee. I was so glad to see him smile when we did that. I thought, hopefully I can build good memories and he will want to keep spending time with his family. We got into an argument part way through the trip. The typical family vacation type of argument that is brought on by fatigue and being in close quarters for a length of time. My husband was unable to come on this trip as he was active-duty military and there were restrictions on travel. Because of this, I really relied on my older children to help out. I had asked Joshua to help me prepare the picnic lunch one afternoon. He could not find what I had asked for in the cooler. I was so frustrated with him, and I let him know that I felt that I should be able to rely on him and he was letting me down. That at almost 16 years old, I should have been able to rely on him to find a jar of peanut butter or the jelly, and he needed to be able to do some things. He, of course, was frustrated with me and the situation as well. He was a good kid, and didn't like his parents to be upset with him.

Later, while still on the Tennessee trip, he came to me and told me (and I will never forget), that I dismiss his feelings by saying that he must be tired or something similar. In all honesty, my kids have heard me tell them that often. Everyone is crankier if they do not get enough sleep. I have asked myself often, if I had listened better, would I have figured out what was going on sooner? But I know that his behaviors were not outside of the norm for his age, and he had not slept much on that trip. I found out that he and his closest sister had been staying up all that week later than I had guessed. I kind of knew but let it go, allowing them to build memories. So, I dismissed his feelings as a product of that. And his behavior was in part due to lack of sleep, but it was also something else as well. So how can we know how to judge that accurately?

Suicide is as much of a symptom as it is an outcome or prognosis of depression. We need to stop treating suicide like it's always preventable, and that prevention of it is the only important thing. Of course, saving someone's life is the most important, but the depression itself needs to be treated to be successful. You don't expect great outcomes when you administer chemo at the last stages of cancer. Early detection is always best. It is also the most difficult. We need to stop thinking of depression and suicide as something that happens to other people. It can happen to anybody and most likely at some point has affected the majority of people you have interacted with.

Abraham Maslow, an American Psychologist, developed a pyramid that demonstrates a hierarchy of needs that applies to every human being. The base of the pyramid is physiological. Everything above it cannot be met well if that base isn't covered. A person is not going to be worried about learning to read when they don't have enough water or food for the day, or they do not feel safe. They are not able to move up the pyramid until those needs are met. It also explains why my mental health deteriorated when I didn't get adequate sleep when I was a young mom.

I cannot say how many conversations I have had in therapy with a client when they are disappointed in themselves for not operating at the top of the pyramid. I would say something along the lines of, "of course you didn't get an A on that paper, you have been sleeping in your car."

Or "Of course you didn't remember the PTA bake sale, or your kid's science project, you have been sick." These aren't exact things I have said but they are similar. It is vital for us to understand this pyramid or hierarchy of needs when assessing our own mental health, and those that we love.

When someone judges themselves or others because they aren't operating at the top of the pyramid, I believe it is because they have failed to realize that the bottom, or the foundation, is not secure, and that it is a fundamentally necessary component to mental and physical health. If you are sick with the flu, you shouldn't expect self-actualization to be realized in that moment. It is more appropriate to rest, and restore. When a person learns this skill, and can learn to stop misjudging themselves, episodes of depression are less severe and last for a smaller amount of time. They are also able to start having a broader perspective of themselves which assists with those unhelpful automatic thoughts.

In the second category from the bottom, is where safety is addressed. This can problematic if there is an unstable source of income, a recent move, or moving often. It can also be something as drastic as trauma and abuse. With unstable income or a change of residence, that stability can be restored easily with a return to predictable and safe conditions. Trauma or abuse isn't such an easy fix, though we do have more tools than ever to address this. In the situation with chronic abuse, the mind does not get the chance to recover. For a child who is being abused at home, it can look like fatigue in school, or emotional outbursts disproportionate to what is currently happening. Abuse and other trauma alter the brain, and is best addressed early so as not to have long-term adverse effects.

One of the biggest challenges in mental health is Post Traumatic Stress Disorder (PTSD). The challenge in PTSD, is that the brain or nervous system has not sufficiently healed in order to register that it is safe. There are treatments for that, but it isn't always sought after or normalized like other types of physical trauma to the body. It is expected to do some physical therapy after an injury to the body, but the brain needs this just as much if not more to heal. Even physical trauma to the head, such as a concussion, can be addressed in physical therapy. While different, internal mental trauma inflicts an incredible amount of damage, and needs to be addressed as soon as possible after the trauma has occurred.

With PTSD, the brain is stuck in a pattern that signals danger to the rest of the body. If you are running for your life, you are not thinking about studying for a test, paying a bill, reading to your kid, or hugging your spouse. You are in survival mode, and your ability to make decisions has become impaired. PTSD is a constant state of hypervigilance, even outside of the initial events that have caused the disorder. From my own experience in the mental health field, I have observed that it is common for depressive symptoms to develop from untreated PTSD.

We cannot prevent diseases, and we cannot prevent dangerous things from happening completely. We sometimes tell ourselves that we can, so that we can actually leave our houses, but we know that this is impossible on a logical level. So, what can we do? We can choose to normalize mental health as a spectrum that we all fall on. Each day, our mental health is different, just like our physical health. Today I am a little less healthy, because I ate three donuts, and slept for 4 hours. I am not going to function as well mentally. I am not going to be as quick witted, or as thoughtful to those around me. I am not going to be as alert when I am driving. And vice versa. Mental health is not healthy or unhealthy, it is healthier, and less healthy, relatively.

Knowing that our mental health will be affected by a number of challenging things, we need to be vigilant in the pursuit of building emotional resilience. This should not be a passive thing. Just as we don't become physically fit by making goals, but by actually carrying out those goals. In the mental health world, we talk a lot about both protective factors, and risk factors. Protective factors are the things that can shield you when adverse things happen, or even if you do experience a mental illness. This is a person's support system, physical health, access to health and mental health services, education, economic resources, culture, and perhaps religion. This is not a complete list, and will vary from person to person.

Risk factors are anything that jeopardizes your mental health. These can be illnesses, loss of economic stability, loss of loved one, disconnect from sources of support, lack of access to services, abusive relationships, etc. What can be a protective or risk factor for one person may not be for another. One example would be a person's religion which could be either, depending on if they identify with the LGTBQ+ community. The religious community they are in, can become a source of stress. In that instance, the community can make it more challenging to maintain a healthy self-esteem, and it is possible that their support system can be lost. It isn't always the case, but it is a real problem, and linked to higher suicide rates among those that identify as LGBTQ+ within conservative cultures. A lot can be written about protective, and risk factors, but they are very individual. I encourage you to identify yours, whether you are currently struggling or not.

While these factors are external, and they do affect internal processes, they do not always reflect exactly how we expect them to.

For me, I agonized over everything I could remember that I have ever done in my son's life. Every single interaction I could recall circled in my mind. Where did I fail to be a protection for him? I would recall the time I dismissed his feelings, but my husband, the stalwart supporter in my life, would remind me, "You remember it because it was not a normal thing. Also, he didn't sleep that trip so you weren't wrong either." He reminded me of all the times Joshua would come talk to me at the end of the day, past his bedtime, because of course that is when Joshua wanted to talk about the meaning of life or other equally deep subjects. My husband would have to be the stern one telling him it was time to go to bed. I would advocate sometimes because I knew how important these late-night conversations had been for me as a youth. It meant that my tired parent would sacrifice their time at the end of the day, when they are exhausted because I was important. And that is what I wanted for him; to know that even though his mom is tired sometimes, that he is important to her.

Months of weighing out every interaction and other things in Joshua's life, I thought surely, he had more protections in place than risks to his mental health. I knew from my academic studies that these factors do not guarantee outcome, but the painful loss of my son taught this to me in a way I cannot forget. We should always try to increase protections, and reduce risks, to increase the chance for health. Protections do matter, but they do not guarantee anything. I will tell you some of the reasons why this is. There is a danger in assuming a person can see, or benefit from their protective factors.

Clearly, my son was loved by many. But something happens in the brain for someone experiencing a specific sort of depression. The connections in the brain that registers happy feelings, or connection with others, is not occurring as it should. You may see a loved one and you think to yourself, "How can they not know how important they are, and how much they are loved?". This is projecting your own feelings or viewpoint onto another person. Just like my son's apathy about traveling with me bothered me. I believed he should have been happy, and excited, and when he was not, it was difficult to see past my feelings and expectations to see that he was experiencing something else that really had nothing to do with me at all.

I love taking candid pictures of my kids, when they are being silly, or at the dinner table when we are having a meal, or even when they are studying. I like these better than staged pictures because, to me, they are real. I remember once taking a picture of Joshua at dinner time, and feeling irritated. He would get so annoyed sometimes when I took pictures, because teenagers do sometimes, right? But I remember getting so irritated with him because every picture I would take he wouldn't smile, at least not the smile I knew meant that he was happy. I thought he was being difficult, and I thought he was being a "typical" teenager. It's so painful to look at those pictures now, because now I can see the pain he was in when at the time it looked like something else.

One of the most important things, possibly the most important protective factor in a person's life, is their natural supports. These are anyone connected to them who is nurturing, or who encourages them. This is teachers, school administrators, mentors, religious leaders, youth activity leaders, neighbors, extended family, siblings, friends, parents, stepparents, foster parents, etc. Everyone has natural supports. It is important to recognize them and lean on them. From each natural support we get something different. From a mentor, we get encouragement and training., and from loved ones we get unconditional love.

For teenagers, I would say that in general girlfriends, and boyfriends are not a reliable support system. Mostly because at this stage of life, the majority of relationships will not last. When a person really needs confirmation of their value and their likeableness, the uncertainty of relationships at this stage can be more damaging than helpful to a youth's mental health.

The stage of life someone is in really impacts what natural supports are available. For example, an older person who lives in an assisted living facility may only have the supports that are in that facility, and very little by way of family. Especially if mental conditions, such as Alzheimer's, limit that person's ability to connect with others in a meaningful way. This is, in part, why we see depression in the elderly. There are health issues affecting the brain, as well as the limit of social connections. A person who is retired may also find it more difficult to be in situations where they can foster relationships due to not being in the workplace, and participating in community events is important for maintaining optimal mental health.

For teenagers, there is a lot of danger as well. They now live in a world full of social media. The access to media is unlike anything we have seen in previous generations, and comes with its own setbacks. One of the disagreements that we had with our son that summer before he passed was about social media. He wanted to get some sort of social media account, which up to that point we hadn't allowed. This was because of all of the research findings that this form of socialization has been incredibly harmful to our youth. I also had a coworker who had spent time working on a crisis line, and they mentioned that they would get calls regularly related to teenagers and social media.

One reason social media is harmful is because of cyberbullying, and another is the constant likes, which is a form of superficial validation. It is unhealthy for a person to feel that they are constantly on display, and they can be driven to pursue constant approval from others. It becomes addictive, and creates withdrawals and emotional distress when it isn't available. It can be a very artificial form of connection. Another challenge is that anything they post is permanent. Can you imagine having your 13-year-old thoughts broadcasted to the world, and available forever?

When Joshua asked for a social media account, he expressed that he felt he needed more socialization, and he did. But we felt this wasn't the way to do it. We encouraged him to text, call, or even use the app, Marco Polo, to engage with his friends. We wanted him to build actual relationships.

With that, we also discouraged serious dating. Some parents avoid this for fear of sexual activity. This was not my main concern for our son. We expressed to him, and our other children, that the teen years are all about figuring out who you are. It is a time to make the choices you want to, independent of others. When you become part of a couple, your decisions are no longer autonomous. And break ups are brutal no matter what your age is. The teenage years are hard enough without additional heartbreak, and the majority of intimate relationships begun in these years will not last, for the very same reason that each person is still developing core parts of their identity. So, the person you believe you love, may not be the same in a month, or a year. But you haven't even gotten a strong sense of your own identity, to know what you want for sure in life, and what you don't want.

Through my education, I have studied the developmental stages, and one of the things that I have learned is that in the teenage years, parents, and family become less of a primary source of influence. Family influence is essential, but in these years, a person's peers become increasingly more influential. This is because the youth are developing their independence from their parents, which makes it less likely that they will turn to their parents for advice. I, myself, can still remember thinking that my parents could not understand all of the challenges that I was facing. For some things, teenagers are more likely to reach out to their peers. But their peers, no matter how intelligent, or capable, are not fully equipped to assist in some situations. And they can be inconsistent. Your supportive friend, boyfriend, or girlfriend this week, may not be there or available next week. There can be a real danger to that.

Remember those pathways? Those thoughts of worth or belonging? When peer relationships are inconsistent, it sends the message of conditional care. That you are only worth something sometimes. And while your sense of identity is growing every day, some days it is more fragile than others. Rejections will occur, they are inevitable, and can be very difficult. I think it is of worth to have a discussion about rejection because it is a part of life, and every person will encounter it. People do not develop depression because of rejection. That's worth repeating. People do not get depression from rejection. They have a predisposition, or a vulnerability to depression, and when the adverse event occurs, in this case a rejection, it puts you in a place of distress, and any unhelpful thought patterns about your self-worth will be more difficult to dismiss. We all have these thoughts of insecurity at times, but we all don't have the same ability to bounce back from them, as some are struggling in the fog.

So even with natural supports in place, there are limitations. One is that natural supports can only be that given the information that they have. Months after Joshua died, I met with a friend, and she told me something about her husband, who worked with Joshua and the other young men in our church at the time. She told me that he thinks about Joshua every day. He had talked to Joshua the Wednesday before he had passed, at a youth activity. It was part of his role to guide and encourage the young men. She also told me that he now questions whether he can truly help any of the youth because he did not know that Joshua was struggling. How can he know if any of the youth are? Or, even how to begin to help them?

An administrator from Joshua's school brought some things from the school that Joshua had left there to our home, along with his school pictures that we hadn't even purchased. I am grateful that he did that. He told me that the school staff meets regularly to identify students that need some sort of intervention, whether it be academic or some other form of support. Joshua was never on that list. The administrator later expressed to me that he wished he had known Joshua better, so he could have been a support to him in his struggles. I remember feeling bad that this is now a burden he carries, and that Joshua already had people close to him, willing to support him in any way. He was surrounded by people who loved him, and it did not change the outcome. How could we have known that he needed to be in the hospital? He did not look sick.

The other limit of natural support is internal for the person struggling. If a person is experiencing a mild or moderate level of depression, those connections with others are vital to them getting better. If the depressive episode is severe enough, the part of the brain that allows you to feel connections is impaired. That feeling of warmth that you have when you think about a loved one becomes altered. This is similar to the loss of smell with COVID. You know what it's supposed to be but you can't experience it in the same way. This is my opinion and observation based on personal experiences, clients who have described their experiences, and also things that our son wrote about.

I remember reading somewhere that when a mother has a baby, her body is flooded with Oxytocin, and this chemical creates a feeling of bonding. When the mother looks at her baby, that wonderful feeling is produced, and helps build that connection. It is believed that this is a biological adaptation that ensures that the mother will protect her baby. That isn't the whole picture of bonding but it does show that there is a chemical reaction or a connection that happens physiologically to produce those good feelings. With someone experiencing depression, they still feel love, but there is almost a numbing effect on it. Low levels of dopamine, serotonin, and oxytocin all inhibit a person's ability to form connections. It is also possible that the psychological pain is severe enough that those positive emotions are indetectable. Kind of like if you just broke your leg, you aren't going to feel a comforting pat on your back.

My son came to me only one time before he passed, and said, "I'm struggling". We talked about a recent rejection he had experienced with a girl he had liked and had been friends with for a few months. But then, with a little more digging, it became apparent that Joshua felt that his friends were no longer interested in spending time with him. We did what all parents in that situation would do, and reminded him of the last couple of social events that Joshua hosted where people came and enjoyed their time with him. We reminded him that the girl obviously had liked him for a while, but it was a timing issue, and that in the future he will meet other girls and have other opportunities. We told him that he would remember this time as just a memory, and that life gets better if you just give it a little time.

I pushed a little, feeling there was more to it, and he admitted to feelings of not being good enough. I can't think of this conversation without hurting for him. He was convinced his friends were hanging out without him, and I reminded him that no one was getting together much because of COVID and that a couple of friends had been trying to work out a double date with him for weeks, but they had extracurricular activities on the weekends, just like him, that were getting in the way. I went so far as to ground him. I grounded him from staying home that upcoming Friday. I told him, I don't care who you spend the evening with, but you need to get out. I found out later that he had not been sitting with his friends, or he had kept his headphones on and wasn't engaging with them at lunchtime during school. This is the type of isolating behavior that is commonly seen with depression and other mood disorders. When a person experiences depression, it can be painful to be around others, so they will avoid it.

The withdrawing behavior can be easy to see sometimes, but other times it isn't so obvious. It is a very dangerous behavior associated with depression, and is a warning sign of suicide. It is challenging because it can look different for each person. One of the things that disguised this behavior for Joshua was that he wasn't completely withdrawing from his friends. He was still texting several friends regularly. But at home he would often put his headphones on. He had an eclectic taste in music, and often enjoyed the older generations of music, and recently rap artists such as NF. Needless to say, I didn't enjoy it as much. Sometimes I would let him play it out loud, but when I had enough, I'd ask him to turn it off. So, he would often put his headphones on, and probably was doing this at lunchtime as well. He got yelled at a lot because he couldn't hear us with them on. We would holler, telling him to turn his music down or take the headphones off. We decided that was one of the battles worth fighting and it looked like a typical teen behavior. If they have their headphones on, they can check out of what is happening around them. I would tell him I wanted him to be present. I also didn't allow him to stay in his bedroom for great lengths of time. Because, again, I knew how important it is to one's mental health to be around people. It is important to make eye contact, to see other people smile. This is how you get that feedback that someone else is aware of you. We would have dinner regularly as a family every night for that same reason. Those connections are everything.

Our parenting style, and what appeared to be normal teenager actions, masked this particular behavior. It also didn't show that he felt disconnected very well. And it wasn't all the time. It was incredibly inconsistent. The night before he passed, he wanted to watch gym fail videos with me on YouTube. We laughed at the silly things people do in the gym. He loved the gym, so this brand of comedy was great for him. When I would get distracted by my phone, he would grab my attention. He wanted me to be present with him. So, he was isolating in some ways, and at other times he was engaged.

In Joshua's mind, the people around him would not be affected by his absence. His mind had convinced him that he was inconsequential, and that those around him would forget him. He believed that they may be sad for a bit, but they would get over it. That they would get over him. Like that is even a thing. This is why isolating behaviors are dangerous. The behavior starts creating a negative loop that confirms that you are indeed unwanted, or unneeded, and it is difficult to see or feel that that is false.

A little over a week before he passed, he and I watched *Dead Poet's Society*. Joshua had chosen it and neither of us really knew much about it, but he chose it because Robin Williams was in it and he really liked him as an actor. If you have seen it, you would know that it is a terrible movie for anyone struggling with depression. In this movie, the main character, who is a teenage boy dies of suicide. Later when Joshua was talking to me about the movie, he told me that he really liked it. I asked him, "Why? It was so depressing." He talked to me about how it had a happy ending. I can't remember exactly what he said, but I questioned him about that because, how could it possibly be considered a happy or positive ending? He talked about how the friends of the main character had learned to be brave and live life better. I reluctantly agreed that they had learned something from the tragedy but I was sure they would rather have had their friend with them than learn in that way. I also asked him about the character that Robin Williams played. He was a teacher who lost his job as a result of the death, who had been blamed for things leading up to the suicide. Joshua had an answer for that. He said something to the effect that the teacher would be able to spend more time with his wife. I then told him that the parents of the teenager had their world destroyed. That they were devastated. And I talked to him about the suicide. There was a scene proceeding the suicide where the father was yelling at the boy because he was angry about the decisions he had been making. But there was a moment where the father stopped and asked the boy something. It was a crossroads for the boy. He decided to say nothing about how he was feeling in that moment. He could have yelled at his father, he could have run away, or called a friend, or anything else. The character died shortly after, convinced that his father would always be disappointed and that life would never get better.

These are the things that I talked to Joshua about. I was confused by his interpretation of the movie, but he didn't disagree with the thoughts that I shared about it. I do not understand why, in that moment, Joshua couldn't tell me that he related to the main character, and hoped that everyone would be ok without him.

This is why natural supports are only as protective as the person is able to engage in those supports. One of the most encouraging cases I have observed of this, was an individual who had schizoaffective disorder. There is a difference between this and Schizophrenia. I am going to oversimplify it by saying that both experience psychosis, which is sensory hallucinations, and/or delusional thinking, like paranoia, but this disorder also contains a significant mood component, such as depressive symptoms. That's not to say someone with Schizophrenia wont experience depression, but the pattern can be more frequent and prevalent in schizoaffective disorder.

So, the individual had a diagnosis of schizoaffective disorder, and worked full time assisting others with mental health challenges. How were they able to do this with such a challenging disorder? A significant part of the answer lies in their use of natural supports. I went to a training session where this person spoke about how they had four people who were trusted to help them. These people were their most trusted sources of support. If the individual woke up and the sky had changed to red, or something else out of the norm happened, they would call someone on that list, and have them look out their window to confirm or deny that they saw the same thing. And then they made the choice to trust that person. If they could not, they then would call the other three. If all three said the same thing, they would choose to carry on with their day despite the sky being red. Their use of that natural support did not change their reality. It did not change the color of the sky for them, but it did give them some courage to be able to go to work. If paranoia would set in, the same pattern would be followed. If they believed they were in danger, they would have check-ins with their supports. Those sources of support didn't call them crazy, and didn't invalidate their experience. They understood their role was to be a checkpoint or anchor.

This can work similar with depression. Due to the various medical issues that can bring on depressive symptoms for me, I have learned some of the reasons for an onset. Two of them being seasonal affective disorder (SAD), and polycystic ovary syndrome (PCOS). But I have had enough episodes to have learned my patterns and how my symptoms progress. I have learned to rate my symptoms on a scale of 1 to 10. 1 is almost no symptoms, and 10 is I need to be hospitalized. Fortunately, at this time, I have never experienced depression severe enough to experience a hospitalization, but that is in part because of this rating system, and my use of natural supports. Usually, symptoms become noticeable to me when I am at about a 3. At this point, I notify my husband, who is my trusted person. I tell him, not because I need him to do anything at that point, necessarily, but so that he can encourage me in the things I need to do for myself. It also becomes a checkpoint.

Going back to FIDO (frequency, intensity, duration, and onset), that was discussed in Chapter 2, the duration is important. Because when you sit at a 3 for a week, two weeks, or more, it can slowly increase up that scale. And you don't know how long it has been. Normal dips in mood are ok, but if they last for weeks at a time, it is time to evaluate if they are getting worse or if something else is going on. I cannot stress enough how difficult it is to tell time when experiencing depressive symptoms. A day can become a week, and when it's been weeks, you can no longer remember being at a 0-1, and that can be dangerous.

This kind of relationship with a support person is a contract of sorts. Each person clearly knows what their responsibility is. For me, it requires honesty of my experience which can be a vulnerable position to be in. I have to be able to trust that my person will remember me at my best, and that they will be capable of reminding me. When I tell my husband, "Hey, just so you know I am experiencing symptoms. Please check in with me in a few days, or every few days,", it requires him to be dependable. He is acting as my memory in this specific situation. I can also keep a journal of these symptoms, and that can be effective as well. But I find that having an outside source is extremely helpful in reducing the negative impact of symptoms, as they can talk about those with you.

There have been several times that I have fallen into a funk that included foggy thinking and depressed mood, and I forgot I had recently taken a medication I usually have adverse side effects from. Certain types of medications can produce depressive symptoms for some. For me, I am highly sensitive to antihistamines, and if I take more than a couple doses, my mood will plummet quickly. This lack of ability to remember the duration of symptoms is kind of like when you take a medicine that causes
drowsiness, but then you are drowsy or passed out, and you can't remember why you are so tired. My husband has also learned some of my patterns and can help to remind me of what I have told him in the past.

The other important thing is for the support person to withhold judgment, and to be more empathic and supportive in that role, but also analytical. They need to ask questions like "What is different?", "Why are there symptoms now?", rather than, "why can't you get your crap together? Or saying things like, "You are better than this". For me, conversation like the first questions, are more constructive and can help me find the aggravator of my symptoms, or even what I need to do about it. Even better is to have those conversations while going for a walk, as that improves mood as well. When I can do this type of checking in, it becomes possible to reduce the duration of symptoms, getting me back to feeling like myself, so that I can live my life. It also gives me something to focus on rather than thinking negatively about myself, because it isn't my fault, though it is my challenge.

****The following is just an example of what a scale can look like. It can and should be individualized. It also does not include physical symptoms which can also be indicative of depression, anxiety, or other disorders.

Depression Scale	Symptoms	Personal Actions	Support
1	Little or no symptoms with some down days, but hopeful things will get better	Spending time with others, active, nutrition, practice good sleep hygiene	
2			
3			
4	More than ½ or the days are down, feeling hopeless, low-self worth	Will let support people know that the level is a 4.	Check in regularly for a number
5	More brain fog, difficulty concentrating, disinterest in doing things, moving slower, or restlessness	Make an appointment with a physician or mental health professional	Provide encouragement
6	Loneliness, hopelessness, low self-esteem, difficulty sleeping or sleeping more often than normal, irritable, zoned out, and disconnected.		
7	Isolating behaviors. Beginning to have suicidal ideation. Includes all previous symptoms		
8	Passive suicidal ideation – thoughts: "I would be better off dead, or other would be better if I was gone."		Schedule with therapist and/or doctor to review medications
9	Starting to think of methods or plans	Will go to the ER.	Go with them.
10	Has intention to act on plan of suicide.		

Unseen: challenges in treatment

There are so many conversations that I recall having with Joshua about mental health. He had more knowledge than the average person. I remember talking to him about our neighbor who had passed from suicide in April 2020. We hadn't told any of the children, not wanting to give them one more thing to worry about during the pandemic. But it came up in conversation within a month or two before Joshua passed away. He said all of the right things. He even said, "I know Mom. It's a permanent solution to a temporary problem." I hadn't actually used that phrase with him as I know that someone in a depressive episode does not experience that as a temporary thing believing that it will ever get better. I do remember telling him that we can never tell who is just hanging on, so we need to be kind to everyone in all of our interactions. Even when setting boundaries with others, we can be firm, but kind. Though I knew from my work experience that any person could be vulnerable to depression and suicide, I did not know that during this timeframe, he had been battling those suicidal thoughts. It is painful to think that during these conversations, he never said a thing. Why couldn't he have said, "That's me! I am the one! Help Me!". Oh, how I wish he would have. So why didn't (or couldn't) he? Why do people suffer in silence?

When Joshua was about 2 years old, I noticed something was off. It was so subtle, that most would not notice, but even though I was a young mom, I was very attentive. I paid attention to all the little things. Joshua loved reading books with me, and I had illustrated flashcards to teach him words when he was learning to speak. I would have to hide those cards at times because if he found them, he would want to "read" them with me many times a day, and really, I would reach my limit after about the fourth time.

I had the cute wooden puzzles with the alphabet and numbers on them. These were supposed to be good for developing motor skills while working on letter and number identification. Between 2 and 3- years old he had more than half of the letters memorized. I would work on numbers, but that wasn't the favorite for either of us. I worked on colors and shapes with him as well. He was bright, and I had no explanation why he struggled to name the colors. He would be inconsistent with what he would call them. After a while, I told my husband that I believed our son was color blind. My husband dismissed this as more of an anxiety of a mom than something to actually worry about. I was adamant that something was off. In my mind colors were far easier than letters, and my son struggled with them.

Though I worried about it, it didn't seem to affect him much. Sometimes the colors he would choose for an art project didn't make sense, like selecting the color purple for faces. But other than the odd thing here or there it didn't really seem to impact him all that much in day-to-day things. It wasn't until several years later on a road trip that my husband was asking him what color pencil he wanted to draw with and he realized that Joshua was too old to not know his colors. He would mislabel them the majority of the time. It was clear that he was guessing. At about 7 or 8 years of age, he received a color deficiency diagnosis from the family eye doctor. It was considered a "significant color deficiency". We made jokes about how he would not be an interior designer or the guy on the bomb squad, because really as far as life challenges go, a color deficiency seemed so mild. There were a few areas it did affect him however. I was worried about him when he was learning to drive, but he seemed to do ok. That seemed to be more my worry

UNSEEN: CHALLENGES IN TREATMENT

than an actual challenge. When he would help in the kitchen, he would have to ask someone to check the meat to see if it was done. But before that, he would argue with us about colors.

Every school year, I would let him choose a new t-shirt for the first day of school. Something "funny", or "cool". One year he chose a hot pink shirt that said, "Tough guys wear pink.". He went through a phase where pink was his favorite color. I asked him if it counted because he couldn't see pink. He got so mad at me whenever I would say something like that. He would exclaim, "I know what pink is!", like somehow his intelligence was being questioned. We tried to explain to him that we know he can identify what pink is, but he is not seeing what those with full spectrum vision are seeing. His world was more neutral. But you could not convince him. As he got older, he was more receptive to help in areas where color impacted him, but it was still a sensitive subject.

I remember sitting with another eye doctor, maybe when Joshua was 13 or 14, and she showed me a picture of what scientist believe those with his color deficiency see. It hit me so hard, and I got a bit emotional. It was the first time that I realized that Joshua wasn't able to enjoy the world in the same way that I can. No wonder he didn't care for fall pictures. Other than the bright yellows, everything else was varying shades of blah. Because red and green are more than red and green. They are purples, and browns, and everything in between. On the outside, you would not recognize that he could not see those things. And for Joshua, he did not know what he could not see. I had asked him if he wanted full spectrum color glasses, and he told me he didn't care because he didn't really notice that he was missing anything.

UNSEEN: CHALLENGES IN TREATMENT

I would think about that a lot after his death. To everyone else, he seemed a smart, funny, kind, joyful person, but he wasn't experiencing his world in full color. Mental illness is this way. We cannot always see it on the outside. Even with me paying attention to the small things, it took years for Joshua to be diagnosed with a color deficiency. And he didn't accept something was different for him for several years after that.

UNSEEN: CHALLENGES IN TREATMENT

How often do people live with mental illness for years and years, because they believe that their experience is reality? Their world is darker, but it is what they are used to. Telling someone that going to the doctor will make things different doesn't always compute because their reality is real to them and they don't even know how things can be different. How do you describe the blue sky to someone who has never seen it?

In my work as a mental health therapist, I have worked primarily with adults who were chronically ill, because the disorders they face are more complicated and resistant to treatment. Because of that, my clients typically had a diminished ability to work fulltime, or participate fully in their communities. My work focused on getting to the point in treatment where symptoms were reduced, and the client could live a fulfilling life while being able to be a part of their community. The idea is that, even the person who is easily overlooked has something of worth to bring to those around them. Despite severe mental illness, they have gifts and unique talents to show the world.

The adults I worked with had a range of mental health diagnoses including depression, anxiety, bipolar, schizoaffective, and schizophrenic disorders, with co-occurring health diagnoses and substance use. I want to describe what it is like to work with someone with schizophrenia. Just like depression, schizophrenia can look very different from person to person. The qualifying symptoms must be there for a diagnosis to be given, but each person's experience is unique, so we aren't just treating a disease, we are giving treatment to a person.

I am going to describe some examples based on my experience. While the descriptions are described as an individual, they aren't a particular person, and are characteristic of multiple people with the same condition. The best case, or more functional case of schizophrenia that I observed was an individual who was very good at camouflaging their symptoms. They knew that if they were to respond to their hallucinations, that people could mistreat them, so they adapted. They were able to be consistent with taking medications, and it helped tremendously. The medication reduced the fog. They were, at times, able to recognize that what they saw or heard may not be what another person did. They were also able to engage in "reality checks,", where they would share their current experience with a trusted person. They were able to discuss things they were seeing, or hearing, and express at times, suspicion that those things may not be real, though they were not certain. On the outside, you could not guess what this person was experiencing, but, if you knew what this person was diagnosed with, you would also notice that when you asked a question, they would pause and look away. Not in a way that they are thinking about your question, but there are other stimulations, visions, or noises that are also taking place simultaneously to that conversation. Kind of like having a TV running in the background while you are trying to focus on the conversation. But instead of a TV it could be someone calling your name, a giant spider or alien looking in the window, or other irregular things.

Imagine for a minute, how difficult that would be to live with. We all have moments where our mind plays tricks on us. Maybe we see someone in the dark and then realize that it is just a lamp. Our minds are tricked for a second, but we are able to reason it out and look for more evidence to either authenticate our vision or disprove it. A person who lives with schizophrenia does not have that luxury.

Another example is of the worst types of cases that I have observed, which is describe as an individual, but multiple people could match a similar description of this condition. The individual in this example, experienced psychosis with auditory hallucinations and paranoia. This manifested as a group of people that were tormenting them. This group would yell at the person at all hours of the day. They would yell obscenities, and taunt the individual about their most vulnerable experiences and insecurities. Really, it was just the worst kind of bullying. It really was tormenting, and that was that person's daily reality. If you were to ask anybody around that person however, they would say they didn't hear those voices, and that they had not seen any person harassing that individual. The individual with psychosis had also learned to mask their symptoms, not because they had any suspicion that this wasn't reality, but because they didn't want people to "lock them away", or to suffer other potentially negative outcomes. If you were to ask them why another person does not hear what they are hearing, they would tell you, "That is because the people who yell have left for a while.". And the person would become very agitated that no one would believe them. The person with the condition would wonder, why couldn't someone just call the cops and have those people taken away? Because they were just so tired of the constant barraging and negative verbal assault. They were tired of their feelings of safety, self-worth, and hope for better things being beaten down. You see those "people" sounded a lot like the inner voices we all have when our self-talk becomes negative. Every fear that we have of the world, and every fear of our own inadequacies, come to life in psychosis. Take the bullying that we see in the youth these days, and the severity of some of the cases, where a person is truly beaten down, and ends up in a state of deep depression. Now imagine that there is nowhere that you can go to escape it. Often individuals that I had worked with would have "tormentors,", or "stalkers,", that would follow them everywhere they went in life.

This is their reality. It used to be considered best practice to confront the visual or auditory hallucinations or delusions, but almost always this causes distress for that person. It is distressing because you are telling them their world does not exist, so for them they are facing a scary reality where they cannot trust their own mind. If they can't trust their own mind, how will they know where the dangers are? Though it might be silly, I think of the movie, The Matrix. There is a moment where the main character has a chance to choose to go back to one reality or accept a new one. How difficult of a choice would that be? And there is no guarantee that this new existence is better.

It seems like a stretch to go from schizophrenia to depression, but with all the people I have observed, I have noticed this idea of altered perspective, or delusional beliefs. When a person's reality is dark and they cannot see that things will get better, or they believe they would be better off dead, and perhaps everyone in their life would be better off without them, are these not delusional beliefs? Is there a reality where things will never get better? We know this to be false because the future holds both good and bad things; challenges and successes. We know that every winter will turn to spring, and every night will turn to day. We also know that if someone we love is suffering from depression, they are not a burden, and we are all better off if those with suicidal ideation stay in our lives.

The altered reality of depression becomes so prevalent, that it becomes incredibly difficult to view the world, those around you, and yourself with clarity. When I experienced postpartum depression, my mind became convinced that my husband and kids would be ok without me. They would be better off if Jon married someone who didn't feel the way I felt, and the kids would be better with a mom who could be happy. I never got so bad that I had active suicidal thoughts, but I remember those thoughts and feelings being so real to me. You could not convince me otherwise. My husband would reassure me that he loved me and that he was lucky to have me, but it was so false in my mind. I was convinced he didn't know the truth of it, and that how I felt was more accurate. My mind would work around his reassurances very easily.

I hated feeling and thinking that way, and yet I could not change it. Really, the only things that changed it were the treatment of the medical issues preventing me from sleeping, and time. Even after the medical issues were resolved, it took months to make a full recovery from the depression. Like a heavy blanket that you gradually pull off, you don't start out feeling happy right away. You start to feel that you can do more than just endure each moment, and then you start to get through the day a little better. You have to focus on each week, because thinking about feeling this way for longer than that is excruciating and overwhelming. After a while, you get to the point where you notice a month has passed, and you start to have hope. You start to realize that you still aren't feeling great, but it's better, and maybe that means it will keep getting better. You can get showered and go to a playdate with your kids without feeling so awful. You notice that you are able to clean your whole house because your energy is coming back. You start to feel better about yourself because you are able to do the things you used to do when you felt like yourself. It continues until you have a realization one day, that you can't remember the last time you had to just make it through the day. You begin to think more about what you are looking forward to in life. You don't know exactly when it happened, but you can look back on the worst of it, and still feel a shadow of that pain, but you are so grateful not to be there anymore.

I have heard people call depression a pit, something you have to climb out of, if you can. Sometimes you need help. Most of the time you need help. But that makes it difficult, because not many people like to ask for help. This is 1000 times worse than going to the doctor for a boil on your butt, as far as the level of vulnerability. I mean, I don't have the exact numbers, and I've never had a boil on my butt, but you understand my point. This is especially difficult when you are a teenager and you believe that you should be strong enough, or capable enough, to handle your own stuff, right? I imagine this is sometimes a barrier for men as well. Even if a woman doesn't go to a professional for help, they are more likely to talk about things with their friends and look for support. Postpartum depression carries less stigma now than when my mother was having children, and it has become more acceptable to talk about within those circles of friends.

There was a reason that Joshua was never on an intervention list at school. He did not display behaviors that justified that level of attention. Similarly, at home, we had concerns for him, as with all of our children, and we addressed what we saw. We encouraged him in the things he was doing. We told him it is a difficult time in the world, and a difficult season of life, but that things will get better. We spent regular time with him. Had we known what symptoms he was experiencing, we would have dropped everything and taken him to the hospital. It is impossible not to run through the things that happened that night, and identify any number of things that I could have done differently, that would have kept him here with us. I know others in Joshua's life experience that as well. I truly believe that the illness had progressed to a point where anything short of hospitalization and medication, would not have saved him. And there is no guarantee that that would have done more than buy him some time. We will never know if he would have been one of the cases where the person was saved and lived a long life afterwards. And that haunts us.

The question that I have is, why do we not screen all teenagers? If this is the second leading cause of death for this age group, why are we not treating it like the threat it is? Hopefully, I have done an adequate job of explaining why it is difficult for a person experiencing their first episode of depression to self-diagnose and ask for help. So why are we relying on self-report as the primary means of diagnosis and intervention? I believe this is a large part of why this disease is the second leading cause of death for this age group.

Last year, we, as parents, had to do a daily screening for COVID for our children on an app that the school district had developed. It was a clever and simple way to screen everyone. Every year my children are required to have a medical physical to participate in sports. Sometimes those well-checks include a basic depression screening, as well as a question about whether they feel safe at home. It seems this is being done more and more in medical settings, which is encouraging to see. But what about the children who don't participate in sports? This process also doesn't account for whether a person will answer honestly. I believe that regular screening brings awareness of symptoms. It may penetrate through the fog someone with depression is experiencing. It is worth implementing in the school systems, as this is a place where there is more access to groups belonging to different cultural, ethnic, and economic backgrounds.

One of the many things that is difficult to deal with is that Joshua had been screened in a medical setting earlier that year. We had started taking him to a dermatologist, and he was prescribed medication for acne. We chose to go this route because we didn't want the acne to affect his self-esteem, because self-esteem is so fragile at this age. The medication regiment would take several months to a year to complete. It required monthly checkups with the doctor. In part, because one of the rare side effects is depression and suicidal thinking. I remember, maybe in September, thinking he was done with it, and then I found one last box of it, which was a month's worth. And I remember thinking, maybe this is why he has been a little more mopey than usual. I had been keeping my eye out for that side effect, and had talked to him about it. I asked him, "Do you think you have been a little down? This medicine can cause that."

He dismissed that connection, and he took the last box of medication. To add one more thing, he did not have a checkup the last two months of taking that medication, because he was being seen at a military clinic, and the doctor was PCSing (moving out on orders) out of the base. That would have left Joshua without a provider for however many months until another dermatologist was assigned to that clinic. The provider decided to sign a prescription for the last three months, and Joshua did not see a provider during that time. I also didn't take him to his yearly check-up in September because the schools waived physicals for the year due to COVID, and I didn't want to take him to the doctor unnecessarily during the pandemic.

I am not saying that the medicine caused this tragedy, or even the lack of continuity of medical care, because there is no way to know that, but it was a setting for the perfect storm. It is vital for doctors who work with teenagers to screen very heavily at this age. It needs to be taken very seriously. I would go so far to say it might even be better for those questions to be asked without a parent present, as teens are less likely to answer truthfully in order to protect someone they love. I like the idea of an app or online screener, as that appeals to this generation where they are braver behind a screen. There is more than one free online app for the PHQ-9 that anyone can use to monitor their own mental health.

I don't know what the answer is to early detection, but I do know that we aren't doing it well, or enough. Even asking Joshua those depression questions earlier in the year, and us talking about it regularly did not change things. I've explained why self-report is unreliable, and I have written about screening being limited. I will go into further detail about the PhQ-9 mentioned in the previous chapter, and how it can be used to establish a template for intervention.

As mentioned earlier, PhQ-9 rates the severity of depression based on how many symptoms a person has and how often those symptoms are occurring within a two-week period. The two-week period is important, because for one thing, nobody remembers how they felt that long ago, just how they think they remember feeling. It is also normal to have dips in mood. You can feel depressed for a day, but when the dip in mood doesn't come back up, it can be a mood disorder.

Depression can also go from mild, to moderate, or moderate to severe in a short amount of time. It can also get better within those two weeks. A clinician will use this to understand if interventions or treatments are effective. It doesn't really account for some anti-depressants as they can take up to 4 weeks for the most noticeable changes, but it can give an idea of whether the depression is changing or stagnant. Screening once a year does nothing to assess a depressive episode that has come on in recent weeks. The PhQ-9 administered gives one snapshot at that moment. The screening has to be given multiple times to detect changes and to provide a better understanding of what is going on with a person.

The PHQ-9 gives a starting place for someone to understand what the signs of depression are, and to track their own experience, which is imperative for treatment to be successful. How do you know you are getting worse or better when it seems like everything is shades of darkness?

When I was taking a drawing course in High School, one of the first things they taught us how to do was develop a gradient scale of value. So, a 0 was the whitest white, and a 10 was the blackest black. Each shade in between was a step closer to each side. Understanding how values relate to one another is important when producing art in a way to depict 3-D objects and can also establish lights and darks within a picture. Producing this gradient scale of value was harder than it looked because the values that are close in proximity, are close in value but must be distinct from one another. Give it a try, and you will see how difficult this is to draw.

This is actually much easier than creating a scale of a depressive mood, but I have found it vital to my own recovery, and I have shared it with others. It can be very effective when an earnest and honest approach to it is made. This is different than the PHQ-9, as it isn't diagnostic, but recovery focused. It is similar to the scale doctors use to assess your level of pain. What I have found about having a scale to describe depression, is that it can create hope. If you can see you are improving, you can begin to believe that you will continue to get better. Someone else can tell you you're getting better, but what someone else believes to be true has a lot less value than seeing the evidence for yourself.

The other thing this scale does, is give a flexible plan for treatment that the individual develops. It empowers a person to be in the driver's seat of their own recovery. The key is to understand that every symptom is relative on that scale. Person to person this looks different. The limitation of this method is that it doesn't work with an initial episode. There simply isn't enough data with one episode to know what the patterns are. But being familiar with the symptoms of depression and the PHQ-9 can start to create an awareness of one's experience.

Another benefit of the scale, is that it gives a rating to share with supporters in a way that takes the judgement out of it. You aren't judging yourself because you are feeling crummy, and your family isn't judging you because they can focus on supporting you in your chosen interventions, whether it is going for a walk, listening to music, setting up an appointment with a therapist, and so forth.

When looking at the scale, 1-3 is where I consider mild depression to be. At a 3 it is getting significant enough to notice something is off. This is where you need to let someone know or mark it on the calendar. Do whatever you have to do, so that you can look back in a week or two to see if it has gotten better or worse. The reason that it is hard to pick out when something is wrong on the lower end of the scale, is because it is mild. These types of emotions are easily dismissed as they are normative for everyone. Someone who never develops a full depression disorder can be on this lower end, where they feel discouraged, insecure, or burnt out. This stage will usually remedy itself with a little self-care, but someone can also just get stuck here. They don't get worse, but they also don't get better. It becomes their normal, and becomes a risk factor when difficult life events occur because the baseline is already precarious.

I consider 4-6 on that depression scale to be moderate. Life at this point is pretty miserable and is consistently difficult, with more days being challenging than not. You are tired, unfocused, and just kind of going through the motions of the day. You have difficulty being optimistic or driven. You start to feel unworthy, and things in your world seem to confirm that. You don't believe in your own ability to be successful. This is the point where you need to call in the help. At this stage, it is important to be around others, and avoid isolating. Your desire will be to start isolating at this point, because, let's be honest, who wants to be around people when they are feeling awful about themselves. Maybe at this point, you haves stopped taking showers as often as you should. You are getting up later and later because you can't muster the energy to get out of bed. Interventions at this point are vital, and I cannot stress this enough. At this stage you have some cognizant ability to recognize that you need help. That help can look like someone making dinner for you, or just being around you to talk to, or going for a walk with you. Talking to your doctor or a therapist can be very helpful, and asking a person you trust to go with you to those appointments can be very beneficial as well.

At 7-8, functionality has diminished, and meeting responsibilities is difficult. Most days are challenging, with persistent symptoms. With my son and cases like his though, there were few identifying behaviors, and a diminished ability to meet obligations was not detected. There wasn't a point where he stopped getting up in the morning, and though there was a dip in his grades a couple months before, he had brought his grades up to mostly A's in the few weeks leading up to his death.

At this stage of depression, you aren't interested in being around others. You could be more irritable, and feel like no one really understands. Somewhere on this scale you've lost interest in the things you love most. For me, a good test is whether I am interested in reading a new book from one of my favorite authors, or if I feel like traveling. I will imagine a scenario where I get an all-expense paid trip to one of the places on my bucket list. If my emotional response is "meh,", I know I am not doing well and I need to monitor for changes. At this point (7-8), you can't focus well, and you may need people to help you identify what on Maslow's pyramid you are missing. You should not judge your accomplishments when you are at this level, as your perspective is distorted. Making judgements about yourself or others you are close to while in this state of mind is unhelpful, and can create more problems. I advise anyone who is in this stage to treat it like it is, which is to say, that you are "under the weather". You need food, water, sleep, sun, and attention. It is a good idea to put the other stuff off that isn't vital to life until you are in a better place. You will probably say, but If I don't do all the things now, I will only feel worse about myself, and all the bad things will happen. This is counterproductive, and if you continue to drive yourself at this point with unrealistic expectations, you are setting yourself up to fail, which will then further drive the depression. This isn't the week to sign up for extra projects at work or increase volunteer hours. It is best to hold off until symptoms are more manageable.

I am not advising anyone to stay in bed at any point with depression, but rather change your expectations. Anything you accomplish at this stage is a great thing, and should be treated as such rather than focusing on limitations. When you continue to move forward at the same speed no matter how you are doing internally, you will burn out. There is some wisdom to pacing oneself.

I used to do long distance trail running. I read books, I talked to others who are more experienced in the sport, and I trained. The consensus was that running on the steep inclines was pointless and your time overall is sacrificed. A walk of manageable speed to the top, allowed you the energy to cruise on the downhill and the rest of the course. You will go farther if you plan for the up-hills, and you look at effort differently. It isn't that you are weak. You are going uphill. But don't despair, the top is close, and it will get easier.

While this has helped me a lot, there are the cases like my son, who experienced his first major episode, without many of the behavioral signs. He didn't stop taking showers, and he didn't stay in bed. He did have a harder time getting up a couple of weeks before he died, but he still got up and went about his day. He was still working out regularly, which we promoted as a coping activity for stress. Sometimes he was obsessive about working out, and that was somewhat concerning, but not enough to raise any flags. We would find out later how important those workouts were to him. He wrote in his journal that the gym is where he felt best. Most likely, in part, because of the endorphins that are released with physical activity. He was doing that instinctively in self-treatment. He didn't lose appetite till the night he died. Shortly after Joshua died, I spoke to a liaison with the military about the confusion I was experiencing and feeling like I should have been able to see what was happening, because of my training. This person had some sort of position where he worked with families in the military. He had the unfortunate task at times to notify families of someone passing away. He told me about a particular case he was involved with in the past. A man in the military, out of the blue passed away from suicide. He had recently been promoted, and assigned to a position that was good for his career and lifestyle. He also had a good home life, and happy marriage. It was completely unexpected. The liaison had other examples of these types of cases, where a family had no warning. I feel that these types of cases are not talked about enough.

Earlier, I wrote that the only thing that would have saved my son that night was hospitalization. That would be the level 9-10 on our scale, where suicidal ideation is a daily occurrence. This is where a person has a plan, a method of death, and intention to act on this plan. That was obviously where he was at. For me, the scale is to keep track and to stay ahead of things so that I never get to that point. I also believe that it will help whoever uses it to have a greater understanding of where they are, and be empowered to make a plan for recovery. But at a 9-10, a person has what I've started to think of as "Hypothermic" thinking.

When we lived in Alaska, hypothermia was one of the main dangers taught in wilderness training, because of how quickly it can come on, and fatal it can be. If an intervention occurs quick enough, a full recovery can be made, but every moment is vital and can be the difference as to whether that person survives or not. Obviously, the course of action is to warm up. It's a pretty simple concept, but it might be more difficult based off of environmental factors at that time. If you are alone, your chances of survival drop drastically. Why is that? Maybe you have frost bite, and you can't move your fingers to light a fire. Maybe the hypothermia has set in and you no longer feel cold. You might feel sleepy, and your thoughts are foggy. At that point you are unable to help yourself.

With suicidal ideation, it is unclear where the line is, where someone is able to ask for help, and where they no longer can. We know very little information about this.

If a person is brought to the hospital in crisis, lethality is evaluated by a professional. Often a provider will develop a safety plan with the person and their family. This safety plan is an agreement to remove lethal means that are accessible to the person, and they follow up with treatment with a provider. At this point, they have regular check-ins and should not be left alone. Another thing that is often done is a safety contract. This is basically an agreement that they will not act on suicidal thoughts, and that they will be safe. This is specific to each person's circumstances. This seems so arbitrary, but sometimes that agreement is enough to buy time for the person to get treatment and to feel better. At the 9-10 stage, we are focused on keeping a person alive long enough for symptoms to reduce. If symptoms are not treated and reduced, the

UNSEEN: CHALLENGES IN TREATMENT

person will continue to stay at this level and their risk increases. This is where you see multiple attempts, if that is what it should be called. There are more chances that things won't line up in time to be able to intervene. It is difficult to keep a person on suicide watch for long periods of time.

So, how do we keep loved ones safe? We should regularly screen, encourage honesty, limit judgment, and, for those with chronic case, work consistently with that scale.

Stigma, a death sentence

"Life is chaotic, learn to thrive in chaos." – Joshua Burgess (2020)

There is a tendency to combine everything about a person, all of who they are, with the mental challenges they face. Sometimes we do this with other medical conditions, but not as often. We don't look at a person with cancer or MS, and say "They are weak.". We just don't. Because, even if we have not experienced those two diagnoses, we do understand what it is like to have physical injuries and illness. We all experience them, so we understand that the body does not always perform as we wish, and illness is a part of being mortal human beings. We view those with these diagnoses as warriors, and respect how strong they must be to live with that challenge every day. When they put a smile on their face, we think, "Their spirit hasn't been defeated.". We never wish to live that experience, but we admire those who do, because of the battle they fight. And, sometimes this gives us a better outlook on life. When we watch people go through challenges, we learn to not take those we love for granted. We learn to value the ability to take a walk in the park, or even being able to go to work. These mundane experiences seem to be a huge challenge for those suffering from chronic health conditions, and watching loved ones go through them makes us want to be better people, to enjoy life a little more and be more grateful. We can all think of someone who matches this description.

For me, it is my friend Dave. He was a runner, and an active-duty member of the Air Force for several years. He enjoyed hiking, Krav Maga, and a number of other active sports and activities. He developed MS a few years ago, and each year has brought new challenges as he fights for his life. I don't necessarily mean actual mortality, though that is part of it. It influences his everyday life, to include enjoying normal things with those he loves. His condition affects every aspect of his life, like mealtimes, or driving his car. The weather can be pretty brutal to his condition, and doctor appointments take the time that used to be used for his hobbies. Visiting with friends can be particularly draining. For him, he's building a new life after having lost so much, and has found that his life is still full of many good things. It is still incredibly hard. A hard that not everyone can relate to. He displays an incredible amount of strength for the battle he fights. Those who love him still see him as the man fighting in a Krav Maga match. The fight is just different now. I am certain that the physical condition has taken a toll on his mental health as well.

But there isn't the stigma for a physical illness like there is for a mental illness. Humans tend to see mental challenge as just part of a person's character. Personality or character influences mental illness, but the illness isn't the person. Maybe a person is lazy, but maybe they are just experiencing the extreme symptom of lethargy that comes with the brain trying to keep up. Think of the brain as a muscle. Our circulatory system works to bring oxygen to the muscle, and that allows it to work. We know that if a person is dehydrated, the circulatory system doesn't function as well as it should. Kind of like low oil in a vehicle. That vehicle is going to start having some major issues, and may stop working at some point. The brain is the most complex human organ. It controls everything we experience and all we are able to do; every memory, the ability to move, to concentrate, and to make connections with others. The communication between the brain and the nervous system as well as the endocrine system is complex and accounts for our ability to function and interact with the world. When there is a miscommunication, it can throw things off.

We have such high expectations of the brain, and that is why it is hard for us to understand when it is malfunctioning. Here's why. When the heart malfunctions, we can think about that. Because we have at least a good functional capacity to think, after all, it isn't the brain that is in trouble. Just as if your arm is broken, you can think to yourself that there is pain and something is wrong. But with the heart, we know is vital to living. It pumps blood to everything else. Without that working, we will die. We don't look at a person strangely for going to the ER for a cardiogram to check things out. When the doctor says take it easy and follow up with your primary care physician, we don't look at the person as if they have failed.

When a person feels chest pain, they know to have it checked out, because it is fairly common and is talked about often. But if there is pain in the brain, what do we do? Do we know we are experiencing abnormal pain, or do we dismiss it? "I just need to have a better attitude". "Why can't I just focus". We lump the experience in with our view of ourselves or the people around us. We will think, when looking at someone else that, naturally, that person is struggling because they just got divorced (situational), or they have always been a slacker. Unmotivated. Lazy. Selfish.

That's not to say that people can't be those things. It just means that what looks like those things might actually be disguising an underlying condition. Much the same as someone dismissing chest pain as indigestion due to an acidic meal they had for lunch. Easy to mistake, right?

But this same type of mistake in mental health is just as dangerous to us, and to our loved ones. I remember talking to my husband a few days before my son passed away. I don't think Joshua heard, but perhaps he did. I remember expressing frustration because he wouldn't talk to me and acted inconvenienced by things I asked him to do. I don't know if I called him selfish, or self-centered, but it was something like that. I was just venting my frustration with not knowing how to handle this new stage with him. Joshua wasn't really arguing or screaming at me. He just didn't seem to care. He seemed more apathetic. I would try to do things that would make him happy, and his response at times was kind of "meh". Well, a tired momma hates that response because a big part of her life has been dedicated to providing a life that will make her kids happy. He seemed very ungrateful, and, frankly, that was hurtful. So, my judgement of the situation was impaired.

Those who have teenagers probably can relate to this type of interaction. For us this type of behavior wasn't often and didn't last very long. We thought, if this is as bad as it gets, we really lucked out in the teenage years. He wasn't a nightmare. He just didn't care about the same things as us sometimes. But the attitude was difficult to deal with. The thing is, it wasn't an attitude. It was symptoms that looked like attitude.

It is easy to label behaviors negatively. And then we judge that person based off of those behaviors, and it prevents us from seeing the real underlying issue. It prevents us, in society, as a whole, from having conversations that will change the narrative to something productive. Almost every person wants to be good. They want to feel important and accomplished. When they aren't living up to that, we need to spend more time asking "why?" instead of asking "why can't they choose to do better?".

My mother grew up in a difficult environment. I don't know much about it. She only shared a handful of memories from her childhood, and most of them were not good. I am not sure if she had blocked out a lot of it, or if she just didn't want to relive it. She would say things like, "At least I am not as bad as my mom." or "you think you guys have it bad.". She spoke often of not wanting to be like her mother. So, for example, she refused to stay in bed even when she was very sick at times. She described her mother as emotionally abusive, but said that when her mother was feeling good, she was fun to be around, but she mostly remembers her being in bed. My mother became the "mom" of the house at the age of 14, when her mother died. When we asked her what happened, she would say, "I don't know. I don't want to know." It was a forbidden topic. But she remembered it was around Christmas time because her mother's presents remained under the tree unopened.

She made a concentrated effort to be different. To do better. And by the measurements we had, it seemed that she had accomplished that goal. But even when she was on hospice in the last couple of months of her life, she expressed to the hospice nurse a fear of being addicted to pain medications. Perhaps this fear of dependency was ingrained in her by or because of her mother. Basically, she was told by the nurse that if she survived and was taken off of hospice, they would address it at that time, but that addiction was not the thing to worry about at this time. Weeks before she passed, it was completely appropriate for her to take medication that would reduce her pain and give her an improved quality of life for her remaining days with her family. But she was still terrified of it. Who knows, maybe If she had been able to seek out help earlier in life, she might not have suffered from as many things as she did.

One of the biggest tragedies that I face in my work, is when I get a new client, who has finally gotten to the point to take that brave first step for help. What's tragic is that they have been suffering unnecessarily for decades. I have seen treatment work for so many people. I've seen it give people their lives back. I celebrate when I get these individuals, because I get to be part of their treatment team. I celebrate because I know that great things are ahead of them, but I mourn the lost time, moments, and opportunities. In my grandmother's time, there were limited resources, and few medical options, with research in its infancy. Whatever she struggled with was either undiagnosed, or not treated effectively. This is no longer the case, and yet, why don't people seek help?

One of our friends in the military came back from overseas with a diagnosis of PTSD. It was so significant that the flashbacks were very real, and had become a danger. They were given approval for a limited amount of therapy visits. If symptoms persisted, an evaluation of fitness for duty would begin, and there was a possibility of being discharged from active duty. I am happy to say that the military has gotten better at recognizing the need for more extensive treatment, and has worked toward treating PTSD rather than labeling individuals as "fit" or not. We cannot change whether people seek help or not by treating them like they are broken.

We hear the word "Stigma" everywhere, but what does that even mean? It is a negative view of an ordinary thing. So, the stigma stops the conversation before it can even begin. Our own lack of willingness to adapt to new information hurts everyone. Society tends to oversimplify the complex, and to complicate the simple. Mental health is extremely complicated, but caring for people isn't. It is easy to attribute mental health issues to one thing, when it involves many. And because we don't understand, we forget to care about those who are suffering, even though simple acts are what they need most.

Even though mental health was talked about often in our home, I wonder how much the negative stigma affected my son. Did he feel it was unacceptable for him to ask for help, because only weak or broken people need help? I didn't think this was a barrier for him, as we were very open with him. I started talking to him about my own experience as he got older knowing that as a teenager, his mental health would go through a vulnerable stage. I also recognized that mental health challenges were a possibility due to his genetic inheritance. One of his friends had been hospitalized for suicidal ideation and other mental health symptoms. Joshua wrote to his friend and basically told him that he did not judge him, and that he cared for him. He told him that even though he did not understand what his friend was going through, Jesus Christ did. So, at some point he displayed empathy and concern for his friend. I know he was grateful that his friend was alive and with us. He offered encouragement. This all happened approximately a year before his own death. It's hard to know exactly how things deteriorated in those months, but Joshua was focused on being strong. He hated the idea of being weak. This must have come into play in his views. Our views of

STIGMA, A DEATH SENTENCE

others and the views they have of themselves can override and mask symptoms.

Eight days before Joshua passed, he was doing his daily chore. Everyone in the family had a daily chore that shouldn't have taken more than 10-20 minutes to complete. His was cleaning the downstairs bathroom that week and sweeping the downstairs hallways. Out of our children he was the best at cleaning the bathrooms, ironically, in a house of girls. But he was acting more like a couple of his sisters who have focus issues. Just forgetting things or not completing things. I was frustrated with him that day, and he was frustrated with me. There was actually probably a lot of other stuff going on in his head. We know now that he must have been experiencing the brain fog and difficulty of concentration that can come from depression. But at the time, it looked like a lack of caring. This is the text that I sent him that day.

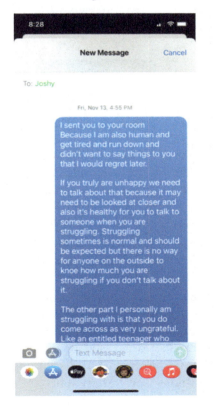

STIGMA, A DEATH SENTENCE

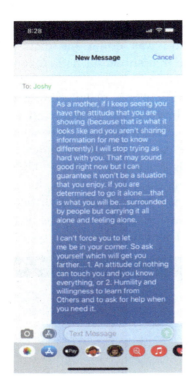 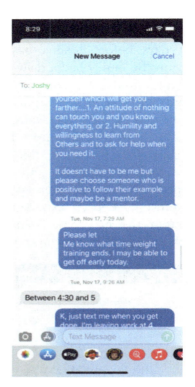

For those who have children, you will appreciate the difficulty we face as parents to know when to be tough on our children, and when to protect and embrace them. We are trying to prepare them for adulthood and the challenges ahead of them, but we also want them to know that we are there for them. And we always wonder if we get it right.

For Joshua, and for all of us at times, there is a disconnect between the things that we know and the things that we feel. An example of this is a teenage girl who is experiencing feelings of being ugly. She feels ugly, so she believes she is ugly. Our feelings become our thoughts and those thoughts become fact instead of subjective items. So, if we feel miserable, things must be miserable, or we are miserable people. This is much worse in a depressed brain, because a depressed brain feels some degree of crummy all of the time. For example, "I feel crummy, so I must be crummy, I am not worth anything,", or, "My parents are mad at me, so I must have failed them, and I must be a failure.". "I can't do anything right. What is the point of trying?" "No matter how hard I try, I will never be good enough.". These thoughts can be dismissed if the brain is functioning as it should. But for those that are experiencing depression, these thoughts can become a person's reality. Remember the example I gave of the individuals with psychosis? This isn't much different in principle.

Back to combining personality with disorder. One of our daughters was diagnosed with ADHD (attention-deficit/hyperactivity disorder) around the time she was in third grade. Before that diagnosis, we made so many mistakes. We assumed she was purposely being difficult. She would be asked to sweep the floor and she would sweep, but would forget to sweep her pile into the dustpan and put it in the trash. It took my constant prompting to keep her on task to get her ready for school in the morning. Homework assignments were being lost on a regular basis. We couldn't understand it. She was so smart and talented. She must be intentionally shirking the things required of her that she didn't enjoy doing as much, or so we thought. There were angry frustrated moments on our end, and hers. Tears on both ends too.

It took a while for us to catch on. ADHD can look different in girls and in different people. She wasn't misbehaving or acting rowdy at school. She just couldn't focus. With this disorder, the prefrontal cortex of the brain is not functioning as it should, which affects the brain's ability to regulate. This is the part that is able to put information together and make choices. It also affects mood regulation, which is why you will often see multiple diagnoses in a person with ADHD. So, years into our search, we finally had answers. But we had to learn to undo the bad habits we had formed. We had to recognize that it wasn't our daughter making things difficult. It was something that was making her life difficult, and it was our job to be on her side and not be another hard thing she had to deal with.

We have had to share what we have learned with several of her teachers who had not lived with ADHD in their lives. I remember sitting with one of her English teachers. His suggestion was to put her into an easier class so that she could keep up with the work. I explained to him that she was tested at the appropriate level and could understand and enjoy the advanced curriculum, and that turning her work in was the problem. Sending her to an easier class would not fix it. I had her clean out her messy desk (the constant messes of ADHD are so challenging), and found five copies of a particular assignment in her desk. She had begun it, lost it, and begun it again. So, by the time she had completed the fifth assignment, it was in partial sentences with incomplete ideas.

But you could see the first one was more detailed and a higher level of work. I had her staple them all together to give to the teacher to help him to understand a little more what the challenge was. At one point she was memorizing book passages that they were reading in class together, because she would get lost and then felt called out if she lost her place. When I found out she had been doing that, a piece of my mom heart broke. She was going beyond what was expected of her, to try to meet expectations of others. She was smart and driven, but she didn't have the right tools to accommodate the disorder.

As time went on, we found the right kind of interventions, and coping skills for her so that she now thrives as a student. She enjoys learning again. She has good grades. Her intelligence was never in question. Her abilities were only limited by the lack of information we (and she) had into what was actually happening. That knowledge changed everything. We did not change our expectations that she be a successful student, but we adapted to a new path to get to that goal and we brought some of the teachers along the way.

This, to me, is an example of how we allow our assumptions of a person to blind us to their inner struggles. For me, it was hard to see beyond all the extraordinary gifts my kid had to understand her challenges. It was similar with Joshua. I am certain that if the disease hadn't progressed as it did, and if we had more time, we would have figured out what was happening. We would have done what we have always done as parents, which would have been literally anything, and everything to give him a chance at a healthy and happy life.

I believe that after his death, people were so kind to us and withheld judgement, because they knew him. Joshua was present, and kind, and thoughtful, and talented, and smart, and funny. He was a well-rounded person with so much going on. No one saw beyond that before he died. And after his death, the community was rocked. His death did not fit. It did not match with what they knew about him or what his family knew about him. That is why it is dangerous to assume only people in stressful home life circumstances, or people with poor social skills, or other things that are considered negative, are at risk. Mental illness does not care if your mother and father tell you they love you every day. It doesn't care if you are handsome and loveable. It doesn't care if you are the life of the party, if you are poor or rich, male or female, old or young. All of those things affect it, but do not dictate it. We need to start seeing every individual as a person who has the potential to go through an episode of depression at some point in their lives and start including that in the education of our youth. We know there are many risks at this age like underage pregnancy, drug use, or being in a car accident. But depression is just as dangerous, if not more dangerous to our youth. Every youth is at risk.

For those who fight the inner voice that tells them they aren't worth it or that they have little value in the world, there are ways to combat that. The first step is to recognize that those thoughts are symptoms, and that they aren't you. Separate yourself from the feeling of it. For example, instead of thinking, "I feel crappy all the time, so I must be crap,", think "My brain is being cruel to me,", "The depression is beating me up today.". This validates that you are experiencing something painful but also identifies that this isn't something that you are choosing to do to yourself.

For those with loved ones battling depression, when they are having one of those days, be sure to watch how you support them in your language. Instead of telling them that they need to shake it off or choose to be more positive, remind them that depression lies and makes them feel worthless, and tell them you see their worth. Help them to identify things that argue against those thoughts. Look at pictures of better times, of things they have accomplished, or things that you appreciate about them. Encourage them to identify positive things about themselves. Say "Maybe today you don't feel good enough. Maybe tomorrow you may feel that same way. But you are good enough. How can I help? Can I stay with you? And will you stay with me? Let's get a milk shake and go for a walk. I will listen."

Know that saying all the right things helps, but it is a disease, and it needs professional help. But you are buying time. You are soothing the person as they are in a painful place and an arm around them may be the thing that gets them through that day. Kinda like when you have a really bad cold. There really isn't a medicine to make it go away instantly, but a good bowl of soup, some Tylenol, lozenges, and a nap make it a little more comfortable while you are fighting off something that is attacking you on the inside.

Depression needs to be seen as a human plight, not a scourge of the individual. It is a societal problem, not just one person's battle. And it needs to be seen that way because the rippling effects are horrendous. It cannot be fought by just the one person who is constantly being lambasted by it. We have to get better at sharing information and resources so we can be united in this effort.

The role of community leaders

**BUILDING TRADITIONS
ONE STUDENT AT A TIME**

Dear Mr. and Mrs.

Thank you so very much for your donation to the  HS Music Department in the name of Josh Burgess. As you know, Josh was a part of instrumental and choral music programs for the past two years at ▇▇▇ HS. He will be remembered as a good friend, caring soul and a lover of music. I will hold Josh's memory close to my heart as the day before Josh's death he sang a solo in choir. The lyrics he sang will be with me forever. "When you're down and out, when you're on the street, my Lord, when evening falls so hard, I will comfort you. I'll take your part. Oh, when darkness comes, and pain is all around". – Bridge Over Troubled Water, Paul Simon.

Once again, thank you for your kindness. Our thoughts will continue to be with the Burgess family and everyone who was touched by Josh.

Sincerely,

Music Department

Morgan, E. (2014) wrote an article in the Deseret News that highlighted a community in Utah that addressed suicide. In that article, it states that in 2012, 545 Utahns lost their lives to suicide, 17 of which were in a small city (pop. 24K) called Syracuse. With an epidemic of suicide occurring in this community, leaders decided that it was time to do something different to prevent further suicides. Jamie Nagle, the mayor in Syracuse at the time stated, "It just felt like it was an epidemic, and we were losing our young kids, and it just became clear that our community was hurting." She contacted both the City Manager, and the Syracuse Police Chief, and soon found out that there were many in the community that wanted to do something about it, but didn't know how to get started. And at the next town hall meeting, a young high school student approached someone at a resource table and told them that he was sad, and didn't know what to do.

"People started realizing how their lives were being impacted by what was going on," Nagle said. She noted the importance at the time with every part of the community coming together to address the issue. "It's not just an individual's problem or their family's problem, it's a community problem and…people are recognizing how big of an issue this is and that we're not going to sit back anymore and will start working toward solutions."

With leaders being fearless in talking about the issue, and community members being proactive in changing the pattern of intervention, suicides numbers dropped. In the past, if there were concerns at school, parents were contacted and that was the end of their involvement. After the changes, school administrators, teachers, and resource officers were taking additional actions and became more involved in suicide prevention.

Greg Hudnall, an executive director of HOPE4UTAH, a community task force for suicide prevention, emphasized the need to focus on schools. He mentioned that campuses are a difficult place where teenagers struggle with identity, bullying, and feelings of isolation. Hudnall described a pattern for collaboration in communities to address suicide. It is called the "circle of hope" model, with three circles that come together. These circles are community connections, mental health experts, and the schools.

One specifically successful program within middle and high schools is the "hope squads" which are made up of students who are trained to recognize the signs of suicide risk, and are also identified by their peers as someone that they can go to for help. At Syracuse High School, 25 students had been identified by their peers as trustworthy, and their parents were contacted for approval to participate in this HOPE squad.

There were also 4 faculty members included and they met monthly with the students for training and support. After this squad was put in place, the high school found that some weeks these students were being approached daily. By the end of 2014, 6 students were admitted into residential treatment, and 10 students had been transported to the Emergency Room. The principal at that high school, Wendy Nelson, stated that in 2012 they had two suicides, and since implementation of this program they had zero completed suicides (at the time of the news article being printed).

An example from the article of how this program can work, is a story of one of these HOPE squad members, who overheard two girls talking in the bathroom about a friend who was struggling, and didn't know what to do. She approached them and told them that she did, and that she could get their friend some help.

Becky Austad, who teaches suicide prevention in Utah, spoke about how she often asked students if they have been impacted by suicide. The majority of hands always went up, but when she asked how many have had a chance to share or talk about it, no one's hand went up. It already impacts our kids, and not addressing it doesn't change things.

For me, it is instinctual to not want to put teenagers in this kind of position. But they are already being approached by their peers, who may not have the resources or knowledge to help. This type of program within the schools, gives them the tools to be able to act, instead of feeling powerless. Today there are 31 Hope Squads in Utah's 41 school districts, with almost 7,000 members (Morgan, E., 2014).

The changes in the Syracuse community and their success can be attributed to the community leaders recognizing the issue and being bold in addressing it, to include reaching out to suicide prevention organizations, and implementing programs like HOPE4UTAH. People want to help, and they want people to be safe, but they won't likely have the means to, if there isn't an organized effort made. As always, no intervention is exact, but this pattern of collaboration is much more successful than before, when there was little being done on a community level.

A friend of Joshua's reached out to me recently, and told me that she had been trained in one of these Hope Squads when her family had lived in Utah. She was in quarantine at the time of Joshua's death, and she expressed how she struggled with feeling that, if she had been at school during that time, she could have helped him. She had previously been in a similar position with a friend and had been able to intervene in time due to her training. I asked her permission to share that, because it shows how much these youth want to help each other. Additionally, she lost another friend who lived in a different state, within a year of Joshua, in the same way. She shares the same feelings everyone in Joshua's community has. The feelings of being a little too late, or of helplessness. It isn't anyone's fault and no one should carry the burden of saving everyone. I will just emphasize again that this disease is completely devastating, and we need to be braver in addressing it while not letting feelings of guilt further drag ourselves down. It is not anyone's fault, and yet it is everyone's responsibility to address it.

In chapter 4, natural supports were mentioned as one of the most important protective factors in preventing suicide, and addressing depression. There are several reasons for this, but beyond the support of family and friends, religion, work places, and schools have an important role to fill. In those organizations there is greater access to people who have varying degrees of education, access to economic resources, cultural and ethnic backgrounds, and differing life experiences. Community leaders are uniquely positioned to make a huge impact for good.

In my graduate program we studied various types of therapeutic interventions and the research behind them, but one particularly interesting bit of research showed that trust in the therapeutic relationship and hope in recovery were far more accurate indicators of successful recovery than a specifically chosen intervention. Whether someone engages in Cognitive Behavior Therapy, or talk therapy, play therapy, etc., the ***trust*** in that relationship with the person administering the intervention and the ***hope*** in recovery were more important. The reason for this I believe, is that if you don't trust your therapist or doctor, and you don't believe there is a chance to get better, you simply aren't going to show up. Why make the effort if it doesn't matter? Your chances of success are limited at that point.

When I first meet a new client, my first objective is to create a safe environment, and give them a place where the person knows they will not be judged for sharing their most vulnerable experiences, thoughts, and feelings. Second, the person's symptoms are assessed along with other important information. Third, is a discussion about a chosen therapeutic intervention that I believe is best to address that specific person's reason for seeking help. I share the reason why I believe it will be helpful, and that I have seen and experienced its success with others, but I also let them know every person is different, and there are other options that can be utilized. It is important to communicate with them that I am with them for the duration of their need, and will work with them to find the tools or treatment that helps them get to where they want to go. And it's my job to be capable in my work, so that I can help them along that path to recovery. If they require a different intervention, one that I am not trained in, it is my ethical responsibility to refer them to another professional, and assist them in getting in touch with the services that would most benefit them, much like a qualified doctor would do. Professionals need to know the scope of their practice, as well as their limits, and they can make recommendations that they believe to be best for the treatment of the individual.

There are many things that have to happen before someone can get to the point where they are scheduling to see a professional. 80-90% of people who seek treatment for depression are treated successfully using therapy and/or medication (TADS, Treatment for Adolescents with Depression, study). So, why aren't more people seeking help when it is clear that it is a need? One reason is they don't know where to go, or how to get started. This is where schools, workplaces, and religious communities, as well other community resources come in to help. These are the areas where education about mental health has the most far-reaching impact. Education within those organizations, delivered in a natural way truly opens the door for people who don't know where the door is, or maybe that they should even be looking for that door.

It is also helpful for successful, and capable people to speak about mental health in a way that normalizes it. When you see that a person you look up to, is capable of speaking about their own journey to improve their mental health, it becomes a normal thing to do. It combats the negative stigma and demonstrates that there are tools and resources that work. It shows that you are not limited by your struggle when the right kinds of tools are in place. There is also an opportunity to increase awareness of mistakes that we, as a society are making. Most of us have heard the saying, "Suicide is a permanent solution to a temporary problem." I will tell you how effective that is. My son said those very words to me when he found out that our neighbor had passed away from suicide, less than 3 or 4 months before he died. When I had that conversation with him, I used it as an opportunity to teach that suicide was not the answer. I also taught him that people with depression do not always believe that the depression is temporary and that it is hard to endure something you believe will never end. I spoke about the importance of listening to those who are struggling, and instead of invalidating their experience by calling it a temporary problem, we need to offer solutions. I am sure we discussed the importance of telling someone when we are struggling. I can't think of that conversation without questioning if we are saying the right things to those most vulnerable, especially as an adult speaking to a teenager. These are arguably the most difficult years of life, and teenagers often view adults as limited in their understanding of what their life is like. More and more we are seeing things like the Hope Squads in middle schools and high schools, which seems to be making a positive impact in that age group.

I remember as a youth, constantly hearing within my religious organization, that I had divine worth, unlimited potential, and a purpose for being here, that was unique to me. It is so important for those most vulnerable, who are often our youth, but really anyone, that they have a purpose. Though not everyone has a positive experience in religious places, it can be a place that fosters that purpose and hope. Purpose and hope, wherever it is developed, can be what gets a person through difficult things. Though everyone has a breaking point, hope has an immeasurable ability to help a person endure difficult times.

In the 1950s, a psychology professor, Curt Richter conducted a grisly experiment involving rats. The researcher first put several rats, both domestic, and wild in jars with water. The results were that all of the wild rats drowned within a few minutes. Out of the domestic rats, some died quickly, while a few lasted several days before succumbing. At first there was confusion as the expected result was that the wild rats would have a stronger sense of survival and greater strength. This outcome did not support that. His hypothesis was that the ones that endured for several days must have had something that the other rats didn't have. Hope. He believed that at some point they had been saved when in a similar situation and therefore learned that the trial would eventually be over. He went on further to experiment with another set of rats. Some he would put in the water and save after they were near death. He would hold them for a little while and then placed them back into the jars of water. Every one of them lasted several days in contrast to the few minutes the control group of rats did. That group had not received the same reprieve and had been left alone previous to the experiment. The conclusion of this sad experiment is that the belief that relief was coming, gave the rats something to hold on for. Hope can literally be the difference between life and death.

Viktor Frankl is a famous Austrian neurologist and psychologist, who lived during the Nazi German timeframe and was imprisoned in both Dachau and Auschwitz concentration camps from 1942-1945. He went through things many of us will never experience or can really understand, and he had a unique opportunity to observe human nature at its best and worst. After surviving he went on to write "Man's Search for Meaning", and is credited with founding the theory of Logotherapy.

In conditions where people were dying for psychological reasons as much as physical, he observed that those who had a purpose survived longer. Purpose is what Frankl gave credit to as the main difference in those that succumbed earlier or later. It is vital that we have purpose in our lives. For Frankl, the purpose that helped him survive, was his desire to finish a manuscript that he was working on, before he became imprisoned. Somedays we may imagine that we will become a doctor and save lives, or maybe today the purpose is to hold the door for someone. And tomorrow it will be to teach someone something important, or to make dinner. There are no small purposes, and each day we need to have a meaning or purpose, even if we can't imagine a grand one at the moment.

We can set long term goals and reach for them, even if life has a way of pulling us in different directions. We may end up in places that are both harder and better than we could have imagined. But we can control our purpose day to day. Feeding the dog is pretty important to the dog. It needs to be important to the person feeding the dog. As we look for purpose in daily events, we make choices that get us to our larger purpose that only we can fulfill. Frankl found purpose every day, not knowing if he would survive the next, and this allowed him to carry on and eventually benefit the world with his intelligence and work.

When I was studying suicide research across the world and how cultural aspects affect it, I came across a study that examined suicide rates in Japan. Russel, Metraux, and Tohen (2017) found a correlation of increased rates of suicide and unemployment, particularly among men. The study attributed this to cultural beliefs. Occupation can become a role, identity, and purpose for a man. With a loss of that employment, those things are jeopardized, and depression can occur. This is not an isolated phenomena in Japan. When a person loses their sense of who they are and their purpose, they lose what they know to be true, and the transition of finding their way through that change can be convoluted and difficult.

We should let people in our lives know that they matter, and that they influence the world around them all of the time. For a depressed brain, this will be difficult to believe, making it all the more important to give that encouragement. Ask people to help you, and tell them how much you appreciate them doing those things, tell them you appreciate them just being around. It is hard to think that my son had started his suicide note a week before he passed away. At least twice that week, I asked him to watch two of his younger sisters. I completely trusted him to keep them safe, and, he did keep them safe for me. But why not himself?

If he had resolved that he was not staying, why did he wait that long? Did he wait because he knew that I needed his help and his sisters needed him? We cannot know how many times he might have decided to stay a little longer because someone was expecting something of him. The Wednesday before he passed away, I told him he could sleep in as it was a late start day at his school and he had been more tired lately. But he had early morning seminary (a religious class) that day and he was assigned to give the devotional. Or he may have volunteered to do it that day. He expressed to me that he had prepared a message and wanted to give it. Purpose. It is as much a part of who we are as anything else.

Though I had experienced depression after giving birth, as well as seasonal affective disorder, and depression symptoms related to a hormone imbalance, I had never really experienced suicidal ideation that was more than passive. But I cannot fully describe the very real feelings of pain that I experienced right after learning that my son had passed away. I cannot think of that time without intense visceral pain. I did not feel that I deserved to live. The most important thing in my life was my children, and one of them was dead. I wanted to follow him. This wasn't like when I had postpartum depression, and was so tired I didn't want to wake up. This was a different kind of pain. It physically hurt to breathe. If I could have traded those breaths for my son to be here, I would not have hesitated. I don't remember learning that the bargaining stage of grief can happen postmortem. I lost 10 lbs. in the first week because the nausea was so severe, that I couldn't even think to eat. My appetite was completely gone. In my mind I believed, "Who am I, to eat or breathe or live when he is not here?" But I remembered how much Joshua loved his sisters, and I knew that their world had just been shattered as well. And I knew that they needed me. I knew that I had to somehow get past the point where I was barely surviving, because they needed more than that. They needed someone to show them that they could continue to live when their hearts were broken. They need to know that they could heal, even if the road was dark and painful. They needed to feel safe. My purpose those days was to breath and to hold my family. I could not save Joshua, but I could try to do this.

You have a bigger purpose than you know and it isn't always what you think it is. We often do not know until some time has passed and we have enough perspective to see how we have affected the world. But today, what is your purpose? Maybe today it is smiling at someone. Or, maybe it's doing a chore for your parents, calling your child, being a positive influence at work. Or maybe today, you purpose is to take your medication, drink water, sleep, and breathe. Keep breathing, because your larger purpose has only begun to be fulfilled.

My girls needed me, and the people around you need you just as much.

Besides a sense of purpose, which is tied to your sense of worth, community and religious places can promote a sense of hope. Mental health is different from spiritual health, though they do affect one another. My son was a person who had faith independent of his parents. By that I mean, that he chose to practice his beliefs and share them with others. And though we did not pressure him to do that, we did create a home environment that supported our children in developing their spirituality. He read scriptures, prayed, and served in his community, and he still died. It wasn't because his soul was weak, but because his mind was unhealthy. I have heard stories of people, when they disclosed that they were struggling to their pastor or maybe someone else in their church, that the response was to "have more faith; pray more, read the bible, etc." This isn't malicious in any way and those things may help, but they are not treatment for mental illness.

A religious leader is usually not trained to treat mental health. They are trained to assist in spiritual growth. I still think of our bishop and the agony and self-blame he went through after Joshua's death. It was never his responsibility to be his psychologist or therapist. He did all he was supposed to do in guiding and cheering Joshua on in his spiritual growth, and he could no more diagnose Joshua than anyone else.

Though a religious organization is not a place of mental health treatment, it can be a place that elevates and normalizes treatment for mental health. This can be done by educating and encouraging people to

THE ROLE OF COMMUNITY LEADERS

seek professional assistance. How much more helpful would it be for a person to go to their spiritual leader and after the person says something like, "I struggle to get up each day, and I can't see what good I am doing,", that leader can reassure them that they are of worth, they are glad they are there, and people are blessed by their life. And, then tell them, "You aren't of less worth if you struggle and there is help. Please seek mental health care. I know that it can make all the difference and you can feel better again. I am proud of you for telling someone. That shows amazing strength!" These are the things people need to hear from anyone in a guiding leadership role whether in church, school or any other community setting.

It is a frustrating thing for me to see people lean on their bishops or pastors for mental health care. Unless that is their day profession, they do not have the tools and are not licensed to provide that type of service. They can, however, be a support for those in need and help them get to the resources they need. Otherwise, it's like going to an eye doctor for chest problems. It is vital to know the limits and scope of your position. This also protects those in these incredibly stressful roles not to take unnecessary blame or responsibility for things they cannot control. Leaders in church and community can and do help in so many ways.

It is more common for an individual to reach out to someone they trust in their community first, because they interact with them regularly. That person can metaphorically (or literally) hold their hand to get through the door for professional help. For most in my field of work, we know that by the time someone is sitting in our office, they had to be brave enough to go into the unknown and ask for help, to make changes for the better. They had to be brave enough to acknowledge that something wasn't right. That takes an incredible amount of strength and courage.

There are so many barriers to mental health care. Some of them are insurmountable. And sometimes even when some of them are removed, we still lose people. Too many people. I have seen suicide prevention efforts claim that suicide is preventable, and yet suicides occur every day in every part of the world. Why is that? There is so much we can do to help others, and I have a lot of hope that as we get better at suicide prevention and treatment of mental health, more people will not only survive but will be able to live better lives.

The fallacy of suicide prevention

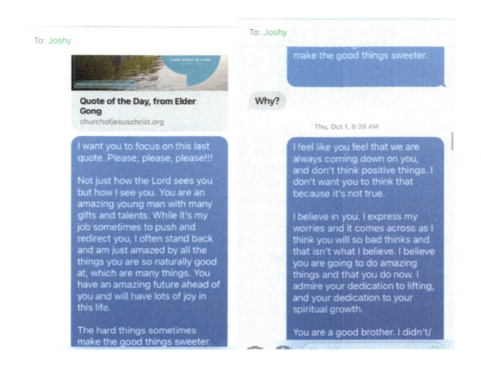

THE FALLACY OF SUICIDE PREVENTION

After Joshua's passing, I remember seeing things about suicide prevention, and it was like a stab to the chest. That somehow, I had missed something, and it was my fault he was not here. Everyone around him felt some degree of that.

I don't remember where I was, but I know I had 2 or 3 small children at the time. I was probably at a park on a play date, and had done some normal mom type of thing. Maybe it was making sure the youngest didn't fall off of something, or put something harmful in their mouth, or wander off. Just an average, everyday type of thing, and I remember a thought that came into my head that was so strong. It was the thought that I had given these children life, that they are here because of sacrifices that I made. Physical and mental sacrifices, and each day I keep them alive. A mother, and a father "save" their children every day. When they are young it is a constant thing. I remember a comedian saying once that toddlers are basically trying to kill themselves every day. Pretty dark considering what this book is about, but what they meant is that as toddlers are learning about their environment, they are prone to accidents and injuries. We expect that so we take precautions. We make sure to use a car seat that has been approved. We lay them down a certain way to help prevent SIDS (though recommendations seem to change on that one often, and we still know very little about that particular danger). We try to keep the children from choking on things, or drowning. It is a state of constant hypervigilance to keep them alive.

Accidents are the number one cause of death for children. Were they all preventable? Are all car accidents preventable? That is what we believe isn't it? We believe that if we wear a seatbelt, it is almost as if we have put on a super suit that is impervious to all things, and that danger will bounce off of us like Superman. It seems over the top because of course we know that isn't true on an analytical level. We know people die all of the time from accidents, and that it is impossible to be vigilant at all times.

You have to be in the right moment with the right circumstances for a collision to occur in a car accident. But just because it isn't random, doesn't mean that it is predictable. We accept that a certain number of accidents will occur. Just because all accidents can't be prevented, doesn't mean that we don't continue to reduce risk and improve safety. That can only happen if we acknowledge that driving is dangerous and everyone on the road is in danger. This is mental health in a nutshell. Everyone has the potential to be in danger. So why do we only assess those we believe to be the highest risk. Of course, if someone is showing signs of high risk we need to intervene. But shouldn't we educate and put in place safeguards for everyone?

As a young mother, I remember feeling helpless in my fears, that my child would die of SIDS. That he would just stop breathing, and I had the thought that I would just stay awake to prevent that. I could not bear the idea of anything happening to him. Logically, that was impossible, but I wasn't really operating on all cylinders after weeks of sleep deprivation. So, I turned to my faith and just prayed that he would be kept safe. I prayed for all of my children every night, for God to fill in the gaps that I could not, to keep them safe where my arms could not reach. I prayed for God to protect them from illness, and to help them to grow strong. And every day I did my best to give opportunities for that to be a reality.

It was not uncommon for me to take a moment to ponder on each child and to think "What do they need to help them grow physically, as well as intellectually, socially, spiritually, and emotionally?". This was a regular thing. I would set goals like supporting a child in learning to play the piano, or sports, or talk more about what was happening in their life. Sometimes I had a feeling that one of them needed an extra, or a longer hug. Maybe it was that they needed some "one on one time" with Dad, or, that I needed to meet them during the school day for lunch.

As my children grew up, I felt that I had less and less control over the outcome of their safety. My children would drive, have relationships, and make college or career decisions. I had to find a new mechanism to manage that mother's anxiety that most mothers have. I told myself that every person has a natural fear of danger and death and that will give them instincts to make safe choices. I had to put some faith into that idea. I did not expect this safeguard to fail my son, who had always seemed careful making choices regarding physical safety. I did not expect that something in his brain did not work as it should to keep him safe.

A regular conversation game that we played in our house was "Good, Bad, and Ugly". These were things that had occurred during the day that we would discuss. I had read that it wasn't good enough to ask a kid how their day was, because you were going to get a closed answer of "fine", or "meh". So, at the dinner table, or on a family drive, I would ask everyone what was bad, and what was good in their day. This was in part because I wanted to teach my children it was ok to acknowledge the bad, and to know that the bad does not make the good any less good. Each day has both. The Ugly was usually something humorous, like, the dog threw up and it was nasty, or the school lunch was particularly repulsive that day. This was also to add humor. That even gross, uncomfortable things could be laughed at, and not taken too seriously.

I remember feeling as a parent, that I was rocking the whole attentive parenting thing. I wasn't perfect, but by looking at my kids' smiling faces and hearing their clever remarks, I knew I was meeting their needs, and creating the best environment for the best outcomes, and I couldn't control beyond that. I would say that an accurate description of my approach was that I was a realist but also hopeful for the future. I tried to enjoy the stages we were in despite the challenges. And I wanted to teach my kids to do that as well. I wanted them to have the coping skills they would need if I wasn't there to help them. Not because I had any plans not to be there, but it is impossible to be there all of the time, especially, as our kids reach the teenage years. Their brains are not fully developed, and yet they are being asked to make permanent life changing decisions. Talk about pressure. I wanted to instill confidence in them. I wanted them to know that even if they made the wrong choice or a less good choice, they had the tools to learn from that and to grow.

What more could I have done? That question would circle around and around in my head, while I was awake and asleep after he died. There was no break from it, because before he died, I asked myself that question every day. What can I do to help him? What can I say that will show support? How can I express my love in a way that he will hear it? It isn't in my personality to do things halfway, or unintentionally. My kids can tell you that they regularly hear me say, "be intentional, or you will end up in a place that you don't know how you got there". So, if suicide is preventable, why is my son gone? What more could I have done?

Added to that thought and the feelings along with it, I have struggled with my identity in my career as a mental health therapist. I had spent years studying and recently began treating others with mental health conditions a year earlier. I also had my own experiences with mental health. I should have had all the tools to recognize the signs, right? I should have been able to prevent it. And yet, here we are. I remember telling my husband that I felt like a mother who looked away for a moment, and my son drowned. It happens all the time. One moment they are here, and then, they are gone. And you will forever agonize with thoughts of "Why didn't I see it?".

In a previous chapter, I discussed some of the reasons why it is difficult to identify mental health issues, as well as why a person might not ask for help. I struggled with that as well. My son knew I could help him. There were many times in his life, when he had come to me with things he needed help with. So many times, and for things most teenage boys would not feel comfortable talking to their mothers about. And he knew that I helped people for a living. He had to have known that I could help. I spoke to a psychologist I knew from work afterwards, who said to me, "When you're in that state of mind, you are not able to problem solve. You aren't able to think I have pain, and I should get some medicine." That stuck with me.

I spoke to a friend who is also a therapist, and has been working in mental health for much longer than me. They had known me professionally for a couple of years, and were familiar with my skills as a therapist. They said to me, "If you had seen a train about to hit your son, you would not have hesitated to jump in front of it to save him. If you could have, you would have." I am sure that I messed up the paraphrasing there, but the sentiment being that even they could see the love that I had for my son and that there wasn't a thing I would not have done for him if it had been possible.

Today, I choose to see suicides that have been completed as unpreventable. By definition they are unpreventable, because they have already occurred, just as every accident is unpreventable.

We can, however look at future suicide as possibly preventable. We do have some of the tools to prevent suicide, however, it we had all of the tools, it wouldn't be a conversation anymore about whether it was preventable. We need to acknowledge the disparities that exist between knowledge and intention, with reality. When we talk about suicide in absolutes, we cause more damage to the communities who have lost someone. We unintentionally place blame on them by saying that suicide is preventable. We are saying it is their fault because they didn't do more. I remember someone telling me that there wasn't any more that I could do, and that felt so false to me. There is always more that you can do. Always. I could have done more mother/son one on one time. I could have been more intuitive when listening to him. And so on. But, it's like saying that I could have ceased to sleep when he was a baby. There are some limits due to our own humanness as well as physiological limitations. But we do our best every day.

The psychologist I spoke to after Joshua's death, spoke to me about a time that he was in a leadership role at a hospital. They were awarded grant money to "suicide-proof" the hospital. That was the phrase that was used. They wanted to lower the numbers, and save more lives. It was a good goal. So, they made many changes to the environment, which included replacing light fixtures and door handles so that they could not bear more than 40 lbs. of weight and removed anything that could be used for strangulation. They made many other changes as well. A notable effort was made with the knowledge they had, yet there were still suicides completed in the facility. Simply removing the means of death is not enough. It is just the vehicle, not the cause of death.

We cannot look at suicide as completely unpreventable either. Some are and some aren't, just as with any other disease. And we need to change the language of suicide prevention. We need to stop saying it's preventable, and start saying something like, "our goal is to save more lives.". Treating depression rather than suicide is more effective. Early detection has always been the best bet on saving lives for any health disorder. This is where the focus needs to be, not identifying people when they are in distress, but before they get to that point. Not that we shouldn't try to recognize distress and get someone help, but we must know that our chances of saving that person requires things to play out just right. Any number of things might have saved my son that night, but how many days before that, was that the case? How many times did a planned activity or a conversation convince him to stay a little longer? Probably more than we know.

If you ever become a member of this "club" that I have been in over the last year, you'll become a safe place for people to acknowledge their struggle, their incomplete suicide, or a family member they lost or almost lost. There was a story of a parent that was shared with me who came home from a therapy session with their teenager. Their child walked into their house and shortly after, died from a self-inflicted injury from a firearm that had been locked up. Another parent had an adult child in their early 20s, who died by suicide 3 days after they had been released from the hospital having been deemed low-risk.

Some of the ones that have been the most difficult for me to hear, are the ones from friends that I made both before and after his passing, who told me that their child had attempted suicide and they caught it "just in time.". One had to resuscitate their teenage son. Another one's teenager had decided to tell them the day after an incomplete suicide about the attempt, and they were able to get help at that point.

It was painful to have a friend ask me, "Why did my son survive and not yours?". I do not have the answer to that. But that question moves something deep inside of me in a painful longing way. The only answer I have, is that this disease progresses differently for different people just like every other disease.

Two weeks before Joshua passed, my husband attended a suicide training at work. This is a regular thing in the military now, which is good. It brings awareness to an issue that has been prevalent in the military forever. During the summer of 2020, my husband participated in a suicide awareness challenge where he did 22 push-ups a day for 22 days to signify the average number of suicide deaths per day in the military, one of the highest numbers in any demographic group. He posted this on FB daily for that challenge. Joshua did those push-ups with him at least one of those days. Joshua knew the dangers, and we were well informed of the warning signs and what to do in a crisis. Joshua saw us support people, and help them where we could. Jon, my husband, has had exposure to co-workers and team members who had experienced SI (suicidal ideation). He has been in that supporting role and has been able to assist them in getting in touch with services. He was able to do this because they showed the signs of crisis and suicidal danger.

My middle daughter, who was 11 at the time, had received a message from a friend that summer (2020). In the message, the friend told her that they had planned to kill themself. She had come to us right away recognizing that she needed help with the situation. We had to investigate a little because we didn't know much about the friend and had to locate them, and contact the police for a well-check. In a well check, the police go to check on someone who may be a danger to themself or others. We spent time talking to our daughter about how proud we were that she asked for help, and that no matter what happens, she did all she could do. We told her that her friend's parents now know and can get help, and even if her friend was mad, they were alive to be mad. So, our home was very well educated in this area.

After our son passed, the thought of suicide prevention training upset my husband and I. This is for multiple reasons, but the primary one is that the prevention focuses on the ability of people to save those around them. What an unfair burden to place on a person. Yes, teach the signs, but also teach that the signs aren't always there. Teach people to recognize signs of mental distress in themselves. Encourage them and empower them to ask for help.

My husband still remembers a specific training with a video and the phrase on there still sticks with him. The phrase "Today we failed our airman." This was in reference to a fictional airman who had passed from suicide. During Jon's 18 years in active military service, he has attended multiple trainings, has actively intervened at least once, and has been around or supported the interventions of several others. Some were early enough to make a difference, and others were not. Treating it like all cases are the same and if we just look for the signs then we will all be safe is the same as saying, "as long as you wear a seat belt you won't get hurt in an accident."

In our specific case, I can now see why those signs were difficult to recognize. COVID-19 created an isolating experience for the whole world. This masked those types of behaviors characteristic of depression and it made us dismissive of Joshua's feelings that his friends no longer wanted to spend time with him. When he told us that he thought that they didn't like being around him, we told him that nobody was getting together right now and he had hosted a party in our home a few weeks before, where his friends came, even when they had to wear masks.

Joshua didn't make end of life type actions. He didn't give away possessions, or anything like that. I can look at conversations we had in the last bit now, and see where he seemed to want to make some peace with certain things, but it wasn't anything like when my mom was passing away from a chronic illness. It was almost like he just wanted me to know that he appreciated me. It seemed he was just connecting and it wasn't necessarily out of the ordinary for him anyhow. Thank goodness, in those conversations I had said loving things.

There was a particular thing he said in one of those conversations. He told me, "Most parents have a hard time not laughing or showing their kids that they are laughing when their kids get into trouble, but you and Dad didn't struggle with that." And I replied in a humorous way, that yes, we did. I mentioned specific times he had gotten into trouble in middle school for just being a prankster and getting into things with his group of friends. I told him that we thought that stuff was hilarious, but that it was our job to help him grow into a responsible adult one day, so we had to discipline him. I told him that we laughed a lot about the silly things he did. I know we teased him at times for some of those things, and he would always smile in a way that he knew we loved him.

Are there things that mask symptoms for you, or people you love? It's something to consider and worth investigating, but I would argue that it's more important to have a conversation and help others recognize their own symptoms and how their thoughts and feelings may be different. Start early, detect early, and don't be afraid to ask the questions, "Do you feel happy?", and "Do you ever think you are better off dead?" or perhaps ask, "Do you think you are a burden to others, or that others don't like you?". As you have those conversations, you can help them recognize something may be off. Say to them, "It sounds like you haven't been feeling good about yourself for a while.", or "I am sorry, that really sucks. Will you keep talking to me about that? Can I check with you again?". These are all good places to start the conversation.

If you are still with me, and if you agree that the presentation of suicide prevention is a faulty message, then we can start from a place where we agree that a relationship ending, or employment ending, or some other adverse life event is not why suicide happens. Additionally, access to lethal means is not why suicide happens. The signs aren't always visible. So where does that leave us? We cannot prevent relationships from ending. That is part of life. We cannot remove all means of suicide. It isn't physically possible. We can remove a chosen method of suicide if we know that a person has one, but there is literally no way to remove every means that can be used to complete a suicide.

I won't go into the details of lethal means for suicide. There are plenty of statistics of the most frequently used methods. There is data to show that we prevent some suicides by removing them (at least temporarily). I would strongly state that firearms should never be accessible to unsupervised teenagers at any time. In our home, our children have been taught firearm safety from a very young age, because education is key to safety. My husband has taught firearm safety lessons, and he and I have both taken concealed firearm training. We strongly believe in the 2nd amendment as vital to a free nation.

I don't even know how to write this next part quite honestly, because it is still such a sore and convoluted part of our story. Our son did pass away from depression, but the vehicle used was a firearm. It would be so simple to say that if it hadn't been an option, then he would still be here. But there is so much contradicting information in that area. Normally our children do not have access to firearms, but things lined up in that perfect storm which did give him access. If he had been on the hunting trip with his father and sister, as had been previously planned, he would have had access there as well. He may not have used it in that setting, or, maybe he would have. We will never know the answer to that. But we do know that it was not a spontaneous decision, if it can be called a decision. We know this because of the things Joshua wrote before he passed. When a person has reached this point, they will hide it from you.

Shortly after Joshua passed, a friend reached out to us expressing how terrified for their son they were. Their son had been struggling with depression for the last several years, and attempts were chronic. They had gone so far as to take apart their firearms and lock them in different places. With one of the attempts, the father had found him with a firearm that he had acquired from outside of their home. The same problem can be said of medications, or anything rope-like. And these aren't the only methods. In the past year we have lost 4 personal acquaintances to suicide, and several others have survived attempted/incomplete suicides. None of them were the same method that our son used. One of our friends who passed away this year, had access to firearms, and medications, though did not pass by either of those means. (In the two months it took to write this book, we lost two more to suicide, and one incomplete suicide occurred).

We must take all of the precautions, because maybe it will prevent loss of life. Maybe taking the precautions will buy enough time to get properly diagnosed, and have a treatment plan put in place. But if you don't know that someone is in distress you can't remove all available lethal means. If someone is that severe, they need to be on suicide watch, in a controlled environment. There are lethal means inside every home.

Within my research over the last year, I have been studying suicide and have found that there are different types. Some are planned, like my son's, and some are spontaneous. The spontaneous ones are those that are decided within minutes of the occurrence. This makes detection very difficult, as they haven't even taken the time to write a note or much of one. They haven't told anyone (most likely) that they have been thinking about it. Their occurrence of suicidal ideation came on fast and intense, like an impulse that couldn't be ignored. Personality does seem to affect whether a suicide is planned or not. A more rash and impulsive personality is more likely to experience a spontaneous suicide.

Both opposite, and similar in its challenge to prevent, a planned suicide can be planned so well that it is also difficult to detect or prevent. I believe that in the planning that my son did, he also planned to keep it secret. Once the "decision" to die had been made, barriers to the completion of that plan were removed. It is easy to think of suicide as a decision because it requires a physical action on that person's part.

This goes back to what was previously addressed about judging the person's actions through our own lens. We cannot judge those actions based on our own ability to rationalize and understand the decisions we are able to make. If you can dismiss the need to die or think that even sounds remotely scary, you aren't in the same mind frame as someone in that depressed of a state. To judge a person based on your ability to reason is inaccurate. That is like saying that the child with autism, who wanders off is purposely causing those they love to panic, that they are selfish and unwilling to try harder to think of others around them. The ability to have good judgement is severely impaired at the point where suicidal ideation is occurring. They might be past the point in the hypothermic state of thinking, where the brain cannot even register the cold let alone plan to do anything about it.

I am not suggesting that every person who experiences suicidal ideation is the same in their experience. Some never act on the suicidal thoughts, while some have incomplete suicides that almost seem intentional in the lack of completion. Those are the ones who may have a more hopeful prognosis, as part of them is still holding out for some hope of relief in life, as opposed to death. For those who survive an incomplete suicide against all odds, they are often not grateful for that right away. In my journey I have also spoken to people who have worked with individuals who have survived and are in the hospital for sustained injuries and health complications due to incomplete suicides. In most of these cases, that person is not grateful to be alive. Their disease didn't just make a full recovery because they survived. It often takes prescription medication and therapy for that person to recover from the mental health condition enough to recognize that they have a new lease on life, and that life does not have to be a life of complete pain. Understandably, this situation can have family and loved ones very angry that the person they love is taking actions that are hurtful to everyone. But again, that isn't what it is. The desire to die has almost nothing to do with others and everything to do with the disease.

I remember when I was helping my mother to get hospice set up in her home. She was in the final weeks of a chronic illness that she suffered from for over a decade. She made some end-of-life decisions, one of which was to stop having procedures or surgeries that may help but most likely would not buy her any more time and just make her more miserable. She had had many of these specific types of procedures over the years and at those stages it was helpful. She was very informed about her disease and knew that all that could be done to help had been done. I remember my father being so angry at the time. The anger was grief, but it came out as "Why is she giving up? Why won't she fight harder?". He wasn't ready to confront the idea that he would lose her.

I share that story not because people with depression should not fight the disease, but to help those who are watching helplessly from the outside. The decisions that person is making, if it can even be considered decision making, as it is a disease of the mind, aren't about you. It isn't about whether they love you or that they know you love them. It isn't that they don't want to be happy. It is that they can't see beyond the point of the pain they are in to think clearly.

Suicide prevention is most effective with the earliest detection of mental illness. Detection, intervention, and prevention are all important, but detection and early intervention are the key to reducing loss of life. Screening, and treating mental health should be a priority for every single

THE FALLACY OF SUICIDE PREVENTION

person. Normalizing the experience of mental health symptoms, and frequent education are key to saving more lives. We must assume everyone has a potential risk.

The last thing that I want to address in this chapter is the language of suicide, and how to talk to those who have survived a loss of someone to suicide.

In those first few days after Joshua passed away, we couldn't make heads or tails of anything really. Everything seemed unreal, like a waking nightmare. It is difficult to describe this to anyone. I still have some of these side effects from this trauma now. Sometimes I will say certain things or someone will say something to me, and my psyche will reject it. I can't say the words, "Joshua died." without my brain rejecting it on some level. My brain would tell me, "Of course, he didn't die. My family is safe, and I am still waiting for him to come home.".

Even more difficult is to hear the words, "'Joshua killed himself.", "Joshua decided to end his life.", "Joshua took his own life.", "He committed suicide.", "He shot himself.'".

When you read those words, did you feel your body or your emotions react? Now replace Joshua's name with someone close to you and read it again. Do it. This is an important exercise.

How did that feel? Most likely it is a shadow of what I or others like me feel hearing those words. The strong feeling of denial straight from the gut, or the stabbing pain in the chest, and the voice screaming in your head that this is not true. "Of course, it is not true.". "That isn't real.".

I will not speak for everyone, but those words do not ring true for me. You know the words that feel truer to me are "My son would never do that." The language that we have used forever places the blame completely at the feet of the victim, and the victim becomes the perpetrator of the narrative. If someone you loved was killed in the street you would feel a fury like no other. You would hate that person who dared to harm someone you loved. In this case, it is the same person, and yet it isn't the same. My son wasn't killed by someone who meant to cause him harm. He wasn't murdered by someone who was violent or hateful. He wasn't killed by someone who was callous toward life and didn't care for others. He was killed by a disease. And he is the victim.

When we place blame with the victim, we do not place it where it belongs. When we misplace blame, we don't diagnose the real problem and can't have meaningful conversations. We cannot protect others when we use incorrect language, and we cause more pain to the other victims, who are the family and loved ones of those that are lost. When I hear, "he took his life" it implies that he had full ability to reason out the decision that was made. In the event of a suicide loss, we cannot fix it because it is final. And the message is that there was something deficient about that individual that led to this calamity, that it is an isolated occurrence that happened, with that one person. This continues to give a false sense of safety that we have all maybe been thinking, that some people are invincible to mental illness because they are somehow better. And it comes as a shock when someone we believe to be all the good things in life passes away because it just doesn't match up.

When we say, "They passed from depression.", Or "they died by suicide.", it changes the meaning to something we can now discuss. We can discuss what a tragedy it is that the victim had to experience that, rather than that they caused the tragedy.

When we frame it like this, the conversation shifts from what has happened to a person, to something that could happen to anyone. It could happen to you. It might happen to you. We don't identify with the victim in suicide often, unless we have survived an incomplete suicide ourselves, it is a "them" problem, and not a human problem. When we use unhelpful descriptions of these deaths, it further exacerbates the suffering of those close to the victim.

Here are some things to avoid saying. The words, "at least", or "did you know?", or "Are you sure it wasn't an accident?".

Some words that really helped me were positive things people knew about my son. When people said he was sick, and it wasn't him, that reaffirmed to me, that I wasn't going crazy myself. That my son was everything good in life, and that who he was hadn't changed with his death. People telling me what a good parent I was, and things they admired about my son were literally lifelines that I needed at that time. Parents who told me that they had always been impressed with my son, and that they appreciated my family, were life savers. These genuine words and affirmations helped see me through the times where my mind was telling me, that everything I knew was false. They helped me to negate those unhelpful thoughts, that I was a complete failure as a mother, and it was my fault my son died, or thoughts that my son wasn't who I thought he was. Or, that I really never knew him.

As time has passed, and friends and family have continued to bring up good memories or things they have learned from Joshua or my family, they reaffirm that I did know my son, that he was a good, kind, and loving soul, and that I was an attentive, loving, and capable mother. It is an understatement to say that these things were a balm to my broken heart. It gave me the strength to keep going, and to be able to start really parenting my girls again. I could live, knowing that my parenting wasn't somehow going to be the reason that my other children died. Because, in these situations you wonder that. You wonder if anything you have ever done has mattered when the only real thing that mattered has passed from this life. You worry that every sleepless night, every conversation, every attempt at guidance and display of love was worthless. So, if everything you ever thought had worth doesn't, then maybe nothing matters and all there is or ever will be is pain. It is a dark place to be, and when those who know you shine light on the good things or the worth in you that they see, it is priceless. When they remind you and help you see all the good, you are able to hang on. And for some they are literally hanging on.

Just as for me when I was desperately looking for something good to hold onto, something that was worth the effort, people who are struggling with depression are looking for any sign of hope. And there is. There is.

Hope in recovery is the best medicine.

In a study done to investigate treatment outcomes for adolescents, it was found that the majority of adolescents recovered from depression with either the use of Fluoxetine, Cognitive-Behavior Therapy, or a combination of both over a nine-month period (Kennard et al., 2009).

Earlier, it was mentioned that the trust established in a therapeutic relationship and hope in recovery are the two biggest indicators that there will be success in therapy. The reason for this is that hope is what keeps a person engaged. It gets them in the car to go to an appointment, to take medications, and follow through with other recommended treatments. If a person who is struggling can find some small bit of hope in relief, they will continue to endure. The road to recovery is most often not a smooth one. It is often a bumpy and discouraging road. But the more we talk about stories of success, the more we are sending a message that recovery is possible.

I find the words used in suicide prevention to be discouraging at times. They focus on the worst stages of mental illness, and not on the hope that someone can get their lives back fully, not just to survive, but to actually live! Suicide prevention efforts that use the words like hope and recovery are best, but often the word crisis is more frequently used. And while it is a crisis, to someone who is in the very last stages of a mental health disease, they don't want someone to intervene and save them from death, which they see as the same as relief.

One of the hardest things a person said to me was, "He didn't want you to save him. He knew you would do all the things you have been trained to do and he didn't want that." This statement is true, though not completely accurate. He didn't want me to take him to a psych ward, and medicate him, though hospitalization and medication would have been what was necessary to save him at that stage. He wanted a happy and pain free life. He wanted to date, to finish high school, to serve a church mission, go to college, and have a wife and kids. He wanted to write music and play his instruments. But this did not seem possible to him.

I struggle with that, because I thought I did a thorough job teaching the kids that people can recover. In November, I went for a jog, well mostly a walk, with Joshua. I know the date because the day was recorded on my phone app for running. I let him listen to the rap music he was into at that time because he was humoring his mother by running very slow with her, and keeping her company. We ran on our favorite trail near our home. I am grateful for that day. I have had years of problems related to injuries that have caused difficulty doing things like that. But my health was in a good place and I was able to have that moment with my son because of my persistence in pursuing the best health I could and because of capable and intelligent medical providers.

I remember some of the conversations we had. I remember asking him if he had any more thoughts about what he wanted to do as an adult. He was noncommittal, and that made me worried and sad for him. I think I had previously discouraged some of his ideas. But I mentioned some options that may be appealing to his interests, one of which is to pursue music education while he continued to work on writing his own music. I also asked him about being a physical therapist, because he liked fitness and helping people. I shared that, physical therapists have done a lot for me, and he replied, "Not everyone is like you. Not everyone tries to be as strong as they can be."

I felt impressed to talk to him about some of my own bumps and bruises in life that I had experienced. I had told him that the chronic pain issues are not a daily problem anymore because I kept going back and asking for help, and that there were discouraging times because chronic pain is just really hard sometimes. I also told him that I have had moments in my life where my mental health hasn't been great, and I have struggled. I told him that I had experienced depression at times related to various things, primarily related to health conditions. I told him, as awful as it is, I have always been able to get help. Sometimes I need to take medication to treat the symptoms, and I recover. Maybe I won't need it for years. But when I have needed medication, or other medical interventions, they have help me live the life that I want to be able to live. And that is how it goes. Sometimes you need a little more help, and sometimes you have periods where you don't need as much. And that's life. It's important to remember that bad things don't last even when they feel that they do.

He was very quiet, and seemed to be listening, but didn't offer his own thoughts. I did not (and I guess I could not) know that he was in the very worst stages of depression at the time. He must have been, because I think that this type of conversation would help normalize mental and physical challenges, and that those challenges are possible to overcome. But he had progressed to the point where that did not break through the fog for him.

The delusions of depression are very good at convincing you that these things don't apply to you. It makes you believe that somehow you are different, your body is different, your mind is different, and the way you feel is so real, there can't be a remedy for it. This is 100% untrue, and that is why they say "Depression lies".

I'm going to express a difficult truth for those experiencing depression symptoms. While you are a unique individual, your experience of symptoms is not. Your feelings of worthlessness, discouragement, loneliness, social anxiety, hopelessness, frustration, and pain are not unique. Those feelings do not make you special or abnormal. Your pain isn't what makes you who you are and it doesn't have to dictate your story.

You are not alone and life isn't all pain. You have worth, there is hope, and the scariness of the world does not have to defeat you. These feelings are real to you, but they aren't all reality. Or they don't have to continue to be reality. You aren't special because you are in pain. Pain, mental anguish, loneliness, fear, and sadness are human conditions, and sometimes they are symptoms of a mental health disorder that is treatable.

You are more than the pain you feel. The person you love who chronically struggles with health or mental health challenges is more than their disorder. Try to see them as the person under the pain, or through the pain. Do not lose sight of them, because they will struggle to hold onto themselves.

For me, when I got past the false idea that the pain that I was suffering from was me, it finally opened the doors to healing. I wasn't lazy, my body was depleted of something, and I struggled with energy. I am strong, and sometimes that looks like writing a book, and sometimes that looks like just breathing through the day.

If you support yourself or someone you love through mental health challenges, watch the language you choose. Remember you are trying to reaffirm who that person is so they can continue to live life as that person. Use strength-based language. If a person starts to believe that they are weak, and incapable they will have a much harder time showing up and doing those small everyday things that are the most important in recovery.

When I was at the most difficult and painful point of postpartum depression after my second child, I went to the doctor and tried to explain what was going on with me. The doctor basically told me that they couldn't give me anything for the health issues I was having while I was nursing my child, and, that if I was still having a hard time after 12 months and after weaning the baby to come back then. At this point, getting to the next day seemed impossible let alone another five months. And then the doctor gave me the advice to have family help watch my children. It wasn't horrible advice, but it was not an option for me at this time. What I needed was actual medical treatment to address the medical issues preventing sleep, and some referrals to manage the mental health challenges as well. But I didn't use the word "depressed", or tell them the idea of waking up in the morning was overwhelming. Because that would make me crazy, right? I believed that only crazy people talk like that. Or weak people. And I was not crazy or weak.

After my third child, I did not experience other symptoms of depression, but I did experience a bone-tiredness that just wouldn't seem to go away. I didn't want to be tired, because I had things to do. I wanted to be able to take care of my children, do a load of laundry, make a healthy dinner, and still feel like a human being at the end of the day, rather than feeling dragged through every moment. This fatigue felt worse than in the past. I remember telling a friend that most of the time I felt like Wonder Woman. Normally I could do so many things well, but it felt like my cape was not catching any wind. And I couldn't shake it off. So back to a doctor I went. And again, I was dismissed. This doctor said, "Well you have three kids, of course you are going to be tired.". I left feeling invalidated, and discouraged that it wasn't going to get any better and that I was just going to have to deal with it. I also had a little less trust in myself that what I was experiencing was not normal for me.

During my fourth pregnancy, I ran regularly until the 8th month and then decided to take it easy for the last 3-4 weeks. This childbirth was the most trauma free I had experienced, and I was ready to start running again before I even left the hospital. I felt fantastic. I gave myself a few weeks to recover and started training for a marathon a month postpartum. I trained for about 4 months and then something bad happened. I was on a 16-mile run and at about mile 11, my body just couldn't move any more. I experienced pain everywhere in my body, and had to call someone to come pick me up.

From there things went downhill quickly. I went from being able to run 12 miles without it affecting the rest of my day to not being able to get off the couch and go check the mail. I felt like the worst mother. I remember I would put snacks on the lowest shelf of the pantry so that my toddler could reach them, and she learned to bring snacks to me to open for her.

Well, it only took 4 pregnancies and 10 years but I finally got the message that I didn't have to take the first answer from a doctor. There was something wrong and it wasn't because I had four children and life is exhausting. It was discovered that I had Postpartum hypothyroidism which basically means that due to the pregnancy, my thyroid had become inflamed and stopped working as it should. Turns out that the thyroid is pretty important, and affects any number of things in your body including energy, and is shown to affect your mood in a big way. It took 18 months of taking medication and supplements for my thyroid in order to feel like myself again. The road to recovery was a long and arduous one.

The lesson here is that you don't have to accept the first medical opinion you get, especially if it is "Well, that's life.". No, it isn't! Life does not have to be miserable. And you can't work toward living the life you want when you are in a constant state of misery. Having people in your life to help you advocate is such a helpful thing. It is hard to advocate for yourself when you are physically or mentally in pain. If a professional dismisses your symptoms, and you are already having a hard time separating those symptoms from what you think about yourself, you will most likely do what I did with my first major experience with postpartum depression. You are going to go home feeling more discouraged and like you have to do it on your own, and that things are just going to stay miserable.

So first we have to recognize that something is not right. I would suggest that anytime you experience something physical or emotional that is making your life less enjoyable than you want, there is something that needs to be addressed. Every. Single. Time. Addressing that could be taking a mental health day, meditating, talking to a friend, or sometimes it could mean multiple appointments with multiple professionals Whatever needs to happen. But the discomfort and pain should never be ignored and it shouldn't be acceptable to remain in that state. There are no awards for muscling through it. And really, that energy will be used up enduring anyway, so why not use it pursuing a better life?

I knew a wonderful lady who was diagnosed with a bipolar disorder (not sure if it was Bipolar I or II), and had issues because of it throughout her adult life. She blamed the disorder as the cause of her failed marriage, because it had gone undiagnosed for years, and she didn't have what she needed to maintain that relationship. She expressed regret because she could see what she missed out on in that relationship, as well as with her family. You won't know what will be lost during the time you wait, hoping that the symptoms will go away on their own.

I am going to give some information on what mental health therapy is, and what it is not, and, why therapy is so important to mental health. After giving birth to my last child, I started to have other unexplained health issues come up. I started getting headaches regularly, especially when I would exercise and I started to have pain in my right hip. Ok, so maybe not unexplainable, as these types of issues aren't entirely unheard of after giving birth. But after a year the pain was still there and had gotten progressively worse. It got to the point where I could not sit on the floor with my toddler which was a huge hindrance.

When the doctor evaluated me, they did a few manipulations and kind of gave the stamp of approval that I was good to go. But I was not good to go. That would be the beginning of years of various kinds of treatments. After several months, I saw a doctor who specialized in manipulation therapy. He was a retired engineer who worked for NASA and decided to start a second career in the medical field wanting to study the mechanisms of the human body. He told me the dysfunction in my joints was similar to what he had seen in paratroopers. I didn't have quite as interesting of a story. I started seeing some success with him, but then had to move before getting to a long-term resolution of the issue.

So, many doctors, physical therapy, surgery, more physical therapy, and chiropractor visits later, I have finally found the treatment that I need to stay "functional". The dysfunctional patterns that my joints fall into are something I will always have to be aware of, as I can easily get back to a place where there is constant pain. I cannot tell you how many times I have started with a new healthcare professional and they say something like, "You are too young to have all of these problems." Well, here we are. If I could choose not to have these challenges I would, but I have to focus my energy on maintaining my health, functionality of movement, and keeping pain at bay, so that I can live my life.

I am sure that the musculoskeletal issues that I have are a combination of genetics, physical trauma to my body, lifestyle, and various other things. Treatment has required years of searching for answers, multiple professionals, and now consistent treatment to maintain higher functionality with minimal pain. Many tears and anguish have been experienced along the way, especially at a time when a doctor told me that I would not be able to run again.

Seeking the best mental health services, especially if you have a disorder, or a dysfunctional pattern, can take some time, and multiple steps to find the right combinations to optimize your health.

For a comparison, mental health therapy would be similar to physical therapy. In mental health therapy, you get evaluated, and if needed, build a treatment plan. A capable therapist will be able to bring education, and skills for you to utilize. Probably the thing that is most valuable about therapy, is that you have someone who has gone through years of school and interning, who is trained to be objective, to help you discover your thought patterns, what is helpful, and what needs to be re-learned. Doing cognitive work in therapy is a process. This is where you identify core beliefs and discover your automatic thought processes, and then you begin the work of rewriting them. Just like with my hip, where I had 27 years of stuff influencing the dysfunction before it came to a head, and I had to get help. My life had become very limited, and pain was constant. It took about 8 years to get to a place where it isn't hindering me like before, and most of that was finding the correct diagnosis and learning the information needed to make the right changes. It felt like a "two steps forward, one step back" kind of process, but always better overall, as actual progress was made. Similarly, mental health treatment can start to produce improvements quickly if the right diagnoses and treatments are used.

There are different types of therapy for different issues. A doctor wouldn't treat a patient with a sprained ankle the same as one who has broken their leg, just as I wouldn't use the same treatment for one person as another if their mental health challenges were not the same. The one overlapping thing, however, would be to educate everyone universally on the best types of mental health skills to improve overall health.

I find that people often are not aware of the therapy options for those who have experienced trauma and/or suffer from symptoms of post-traumatic stress disorder. This makes sense because sometimes it isn't even accurately diagnosed, and in many cases, it goes untreated, causing people to continue to suffer unnecessarily.

Today there are a variety of trauma informed therapies, but one of the most effective is Eye Movement Desensitization and Reprocessing (EMDR). This is an evidence-based therapy that has been around for a long time. It is more commonly known in military and first responder type communities, and has been proven to help lower the distress of PTSD in all types of traumas. In order to use it, a therapist must have a certain amount of specialized training, requiring a certain number of educational hours, and supervision in clinical work.

EMDR works with how a memory is stored and changes it in order to reduce the symptoms of distress. Earlier it was mentioned that memories with strong emotions attached to them are stored in a way where they become easily recalled. With PTSD, your brain and body have difficulty recognizing that you are not in a dangerous situation anymore, which causes your body to react. PTSD is a disorder that creates flashbacks, nightmares, and intrusive thoughts. Intrusive thoughts are difficult to explain, but in part it's the brain trying to fix the event that caused the tragedy. It's the "what if?" type of thinking. The brain tries hard to solve the unsolvable, because if horrible things cannot be prevented, then we cannot let our guard down, and we will continue to be unsafe. PTSD is a bit different than trauma by itself. Not everyone who experiences trauma will develop PTSD. EMDR has been shown to reduce PTSD symptoms, and what used to take years of processing in therapy can occur in a much shorter amount of time.

Brain spotting is another type of therapy that works on the inner brain and how trauma is stored. It also has an almost immediate impact on the condition. Brain spotting does not have the same level of research behind it yet, but my own personal experience with it after Joshua died was helpful. The most noticeable change for me, was that the nightmares were gone, and I wasn't replaying the night I lost him as often. These symptoms greatly impact everything in day-to-day life. If an individual has these symptoms, they can barely function, so any relief from it is very noticeable. Too often I will hear someone say that they are still suffering from a trauma that they were involved in (whether it was a car accident, an assault, medical trauma, combat, etc.) many years after the fact. EMDR and brain spotting does not remove the challenges someone faces from a bodily injury, or remove the sadness and grief of losing a loved one, but it does relieve the symptoms of a disorder caused by that trauma.

Ever have the feeling that you are living a nightmare that you can't wake up from? That may be PTSD. And, it's treatable.

There are many conditions that I could write about, but there are a lot of other books specifically about them, just as there are a lot of resources showing the science behind various therapies. The message I really want to leave is, that we no longer live in the era that my grandmother did, an era where there wasn't a lot of accessible information, and people were being institutionalized for conditions that are easily treatable. I see people heal regularly, with therapy and medication management. They are able to get their lives back and enjoy things they never believed they would again. They have fulfilling and healthy relationships, they believe in themselves, and are able to set and keep personal goals. But it has to start somewhere.

There are a few things you should look for in a mental health professional:

They really listen to you. You should feel that they understand what you are trying to tell them. They don't invalidate you by making you feel that you are imagining things.

They know the limits of their expertise. It is impossible to be the best and a jack of all trades. I am always clear with my clients about where I have been trained and where I will have to refer them to someone else. But I am educated enough in most areas to provide some clinical suggestions for treatment in therapy.

They use evidence-based interventions. This means the chosen therapies have passed the rigors of scientific research and have been proven to be effective.

They include you in the treatment plan process. You should know exactly what you are working toward and the route to get there. You should feel that you are the partner in the process and can voice concerns, or express if something isn't going as well as you think it should.

They believe in you and don't limit your recovery. I truly believe that a capable mental health professional will not use language that is limiting and you should not feel that you are your only cheerleader. If a therapist is telling you that you have reached your limits in improvement, it really means that they have scraped the bottom of their own barrel of knowledge and experience. It's time to move on.

One of the things that has been particularly difficult for me is knowing that my son never got a chance to get treatment. There are so many things that could have potentially helped him and we will never know what could have been. When you look at where you are in your mental health, and where you'd like to be, do not fall for the trap of thinking that it is unachievable. You just haven't found the right thing yet. You deserve to be happy. You deserve to be healthy. And you deserve to live. Truly live the life you want. Settle for nothing less.

How to support & communicate with those you love

One of the biggest questions I get is "What can I do to help my loved one?". It is an instinct of mine to de-escalate anxiety as I work with individuals who struggle with it. With anxiety disorders, the anxiety has reached a point where it is impacting a person negatively. It may keep them in the house, or isolated, and create difficulty with school or work performance. The irritability that comes with it impacts their relationships. Anxiety itself isn't a bad thing. It is the feeling we get in reaction to danger, or perceived danger. But with this disorder, the anxiety does not calm down when the danger has passed. It's like being stuck in a certain gear in your car. In therapy, tools are learned to shift out of that gear, or to cope with anxiety in healthy ways.

But when a danger is real, we should feel anxiety, as unpleasant as it may be. To those who are worried about their loved ones that struggle, especially their teenagers, the danger is absolutely there. Denying this prevents us from seeing the threat. Something to consider though, is what you will do with the knowledge of that danger. What can you do? Here are some tips.

Take care of your own mental health

You are no good to that other person if you burn yourself out. Also, by taking care of your own mental health you are setting an example to those you love as you normalize mental health practices.

I remember an incident that happened once when I was at a water park with my family as a child. The kids were mostly swimming age and given a little more leash to explore the park as long as we stayed together. At some point, we chose to use a rope swing at the deep end of one of the pools. It was a lot of fun. My older sister went first, then me, and then my younger brother. My sister either went ahead of us, or somehow got separated in all the commotion. I had a thought, that I had better stay behind because my brother wasn't that great of a swimmer yet. Sure enough, after he swung out and hit the water, it was obvious to see that he was struggling and unable to swim out of that deep area. I looked around. "Surely the lifeguards would see him". I waited some more, but no one noticed. I was not a very assertive child and can't remember if I thought to yell for help. If I did, it did not get a response. So, I jumped in determined to save my brother. I still do not know how we both survived, but it was a very close call, and I will tell you why.

I was a fairly competent swimmer for my age (maybe 10). By that, I mean I knew how to not drown. I didn't have any fancy technique beyond a doggy paddle sort of movement, but it had served me well up to that point. When I got to my brother, he quickly latched on to me. At no point, from the moment he touched me, was I able to get my head above the water. I do not know how long it took to get to the edge of the pool, but it felt like a mile to a kid who was already out of oxygen. It was incredibly scary for me and I had the thought, "I am not going to make it, and my little brother will die too."

By some miracle we did make it, though at no point did a lifeguard assist me until I had already made it to the edge. I remember being so angry about that. I was too tired to even pull myself out of the pool. I was shaking so badly and my muscles were absolutely drained of energy.

This is a common-sense sort of thing to guarantee your own survival before looking out for others. But in a crisis, we sometimes leave behind common sense as we are just surviving. If you don't have your head above the water, you will struggle to help anyone else, and potentially be in danger yourself.

Set boundaries

This goes along with the first one. With my story of almost drowning, you can see that I did the very thing that lifeguards are told not to do. If they need to get in the water, they are trained on how to hold a person so that person does not pull them under. My brother was not thinking, "This is how I'm going and I'm taking my sister with me!" Heck no. He wasn't really thinking at all, because again, **SURVIVAL**. This is why emergency responders routinely train to respond to a crisis in a way that their training kicks in instinctively because the brain does not function well with loads of cortisol and adrenaline flooding the body.

Setting boundaries, along with the taking care of your own mental health, are the most important things you can do. If you don't set boundaries and take care of yourself before any of the other steps or tips I give you, you will be unable to actually do any of the other steps well. Setting healthy boundaries will help you and the person you love.

There are loads I could write about setting boundaries, but I'll just address one important thing to consider. Boundaries are hard to set. Mostly because people have a difficult time knowing their limits. Can you tell when you are approaching burn-out? A clue about this could be when you get cranky or resentful. That could mean you are approaching your limit, or have passed it already, and need to prioritize self-care. You want to be there for the people you care about though, so you are going to need to practice with this and figure out how it works for you. Boundaries must change per circumstance because your emotional well-being is fluctuating as well.

There is a very important reason why boundaries are so important. The people you are trying to help are like my brother, half-drowned, trying to survive. They aren't able to process whether they are taking you with them, and you need to let them know. They need to be able to trust you to know where the boundaries are. For example, if I ask a friend for help and they always say yes, I might start to wonder if I am a burden to them and they aren't telling me, or if I can't trust them to look out for themselves. This is going to either make me less likely to ask for help, or I will carry the burden of constantly wondering if I am harming them. However, if a friend tells me once and awhile, "I can't do that today, but keep me in mind for next time.". This feels safer to me because I know that person wants to be there for me, and that they are in it for the long haul. They aren't going to burn themselves out and disappear on me. I need to know that the person supporting me isn't going to drown while they are trying to help me. Along with that, it is important to have more than one person to rely on.

Assist your person in expanding their sources of support

How much better would it have been, if I had yelled for help to save my brother? At the time, I didn't think that help was coming, so I did what I thought was best. There didn't appear to be an option. Sometimes the people we care about face barriers to getting help. Maybe they can't afford to go to the doctor or therapist. Maybe they have already, and that professional seemed unqualified and unable to help. In a true crisis, you can take your loved one to the ER to be evaluated. Sometimes, after visiting the ER, it's easier to get a person in touch with services because they are in the system now.

I didn't know for a long time (not until after I started working in this field) that you can go to any ER in the case of mental distress. This lack of knowledge is a barrier. Getting other services set up can be discouraging and take a little time, just as getting specialty care for any medical needs can sometimes. My experience as a military spouse has been frustrating at times when trying to set up medical services. The military insurance requires a referral process for specialty care where you basically have to get permission to go see anyone beyond a primary care doctor. But this is not the case for mental health services. No referral is necessary as long as the provider is in the network.

Help your loved ones know what resources they have available to them. When a person is surviving, figuring out the ins and outs of available resources can be very difficult. There are a significant number of calls to crisis lines from concerned family members or friends, not just from the people actually in crisis themselves. Why? Because they are able to recognize a need and take action whereas it might be very difficult for the individual struggling to problem solve. For me and my family, we had wonderful people provide us with a number of resources to help us after Joshua passed away. I wouldn't have done as well finding them on my own, as my functional limit or ability to think very far ahead was impaired. I am grateful for that effort from others and their ability to recognize our need.

Additional resources include support groups, which can be so helpful. For me, the people that love Joshua and me, have been immeasurably helpful, but there is a need that they can't meet. Talking to other parents who have lost a child, especially to suicide, has helped in ways I could probably write a whole other book about.

Sometimes helping someone to get resources means showing up with them. You don't have to be in a therapist's office with the person, but taking them to that appointment, and using that drive as a time to offer encouragement and support can help combat feelings of worthlessness or insecurity. Letting them know that you think they are strong and that they are not alone is huge. I cannot emphasize that enough.

There are other sources of support, that are not official or formal. These are other family members and friends. Not everyone in that circle is actually able to be a source of support. Maybe they have not gotten themselves to a place where they can help someone else, or they lack a certain ability to empathize. But it is important to create a group of friends that can be called on when help is needed. This way the effort is spread out in a way that no one is getting burned out and there is a sturdier system in place. Think about it like setting up a tent. If you use one or two stakes, awesome, it may stay up, but it will be more secure with more stakes. This circle of individuals does not need to be a group of 20. It could just be a handful of truly trusted people, who know their limits, and practice taking care of their own mental health.

Don't tell them they are crazy

Using invalidating statements can exacerbate mental health issues in a way that makes it harder for a person to recover. You do not need to be the judge of whether a person's actions are because of mental health issues, or because they are lazy or manipulative. You don't need to help them diagnose themselves, or even provide treatment recommendations. That is for a professional to assist with. Please help them seek out qualified professionals to do that.

This piece of advice is almost impossible to be perfect at. I try not to entertain regrets too much, but I do regret the time when my son came to me and said, "Whenever I try to talk to you about my emotions, you dismiss it as I haven't gotten enough sleep." That still gets to me. What if I had stopped long enough to put my own frustration aside at that moment? What would be different? Truthfully, I wasn't wrong. Joshua was a moody kid if he didn't get like 9-10 hours of sleep. But I wasn't able to get the whole picture either. And because of that what was actually happening wasn't discovered.

When you say things like, "maybe it's your time of the month," or "it's all in your head", these statements can actually come across as, "You can't trust yourself. ", "You can choose to feel different." "This is your problem.". And it feeds the idea that depression symptoms are something that you could fix if you were stronger, had a better attitude, and so on. It prevents treatment of something far more nefarious than a cranky attitude.

Now, if you are a person who suffers from depression, you probably have this unhelpful dialogue in your head as well. You dismiss your feelings for lots of reasons. I do think there is a lot of value in going back and looking at Maslow's pyramid before you judge what is happening. Make sure you are meeting those basic needs, and then see if you still feel a certain way. If so, tell one of your trusted people.

As you get used to doing that, you will get better at seeing your patterns, and those in your circle will as well. You will begin to differentiate what symptoms and emotions are what. This is something that needs to be practiced.

Help combat unhelpful thinking and foster hope

This can be an exhausting one. And difficult because you need to be able to do it in a way that isn't invalidating. Telling someone it is all going to be fine, does not make the person feel better. It makes them feel like it's their fault that it isn't better.

Ask questions like, "When you felt this way before, what helped?" "How long do you think this "meh" type feeling can last for you?", "How can I help make this a little easier?" "I don't know if talking to the doctor or therapist will help, but what have you got to lose?" or even saying something like, "I don't know how you are going to get through this, but you are not alone."

I say foster hope, because it is something that is a belief, not an item you can give someone. You can't create it, and selling the idea that everything will be rainbows and sunshine is a lie really, and to a depressed brain is extremely false. So, start with something that is believable. Internally say something like this, "If I can be better today than I was before, even if I have bad days, it can get better".

I encourage people to journal the good days in some way. I have a friend who will look at old pictures, because in a depressed state she cannot remember being happy. These pictures are her memory while in a depression fog and evidence of future possibilities. Journaling also helps you to figure out what brings on an episode, and keeps track of how it progresses. This helps you to remember that it has passed before and it will pass again. This is a helpful strategy for any kind of event that requires enduring. I often say that people can deal with any level of pain, no matter how severe, if they believe that it will not last, and also, if they have an idea when it will stop.

I discovered this principle during my traumatic experiences with labor. If I could count through a contraction, I knew exactly when that peak would hit, and I knew, that once I hit that contraction's peak, it was going to get less and less painful from there on out. I would do this with each contraction. This strategy can be used in fitness. In my experience with running, it didn't seem to matter if I ran 3 miles or 10, that last half mile was always the hardest mentally, because I just wanted to stop.

I try to live my life in a way that I am brutally honest with myself, because I believe that we can't overcome things if we can't see them clearly. The only area of my life that I don't live by that mantra is in fitness challenges or other difficult things I need to accomplish. I tell myself, "It will not be as hard as you think." Why do I do this? Because believing that I can accomplish incredible feats seems unbelievable. So, I make the challenge seem easier than it really is or I break it into smaller chunks or "micro challenges.". If I'm running and I have 10 miles left, I only give the mile I am currently running the attention needed to complete it. And that is how I am able to get to the goal that I have set. Just as an athlete can be defeated before they even start, a person in recovery can as well.

With a person who experiences chronic episodes of depression, the idea that they will have to do this again and again is just too overwhelming and hope is lost. Because even if they believe that this episode won't last and they will feel better, they know that it is possible they may have to do this over and over again. This sort of thinking isn't helpful, and can be dangerous. This is where they need to focus on "this" hill. What do you need to do to get to the top, so you can start cruising the downhill? You will not find the right combination of treatment that prevents future episodes if you don't keep going. But thinking about all of that future stuff is just too exhausting. One foot in front of the other. Pacing is so important. So, if you're supporting someone, just be their pacer. Encourage. Don't lie, don't invalidate. Just remind them to keep moving their feet, and that you are with them.

When I first lost Joshua, I had no hope that I would be able to endure. The pain was so much bigger and stronger than reasonable thoughts, or anything really. But my knowledge and training for crisis kicked in to some degree (through that painful fog), and I knew that if I had any hope of surviving, I would need to find evidence of that hope. I also knew that my symptoms would get worse before they would get better, so I had to act quickly, because I knew that when the shock wore off and the long journey of grief began, I might not be able to think of what to do.

I reached out to those who had been through similar experiences. I needed to know that it wasn't going to hurt as bad as it did forever. Because, every minute was like a year. It was unbearable. Living through each minute afterwards, took everything in me. Every single coping skill I had. I was painfully aware that with all that I had learned about coping it wasn't going to be enough. I also knew that my own life was very much at risk. I have no illusions that I am invincible. I truly feel that the two things that saved us were the support of other parents who had survived this type of tragedy and the support from our community. This was absolutely something I could not do on my own.

To those who are on the outside, who have never experienced it, you have to understand that everyone has a breaking point. There is not a single person who doesn't have a breaking point with the right amount of pressure applied in a specific way. Some may last longer than others, but everyone will eventually break. This is human.

Someone who is in a depressed state is more aware of this than anyone. They are constantly having their limits tested. And the fog that occurs with depression, or the delusionary thinking is good at working its way around logic. So, even after talking with other parents, who had survived, and had been able to start to feel things like happiness again, I did not believe that it was possible for me. They're not me. They don't know my pain. Their situation isn't exactly like mine.

After my son's passing, the idea of making it 9 months was just not doable. If I had focused on that point, I would have failed. I would have ended up in the hospital, or worse. So, I told myself, "I made it from the last minute to this one, so, I will make it to the next minute." It was a test of endurance to make it from minute to minute, and I started looking for evidence of the pain lessening. "Place markers" if you will. I remember telling my husband a week after Joshua died, "I think it is possible that we may be able to go on." "Maybe it will get better,". It wasn't even a belief at that point, just an idea of a belief.

The hope was there that if I had the ability to entertain it maybe it was a possibility. I made note of when I started to get glimpses above the water, or the edge of the pool. It wasn't even that encouraging, but I focused on that, and I started to look for evidence that it was getting a little bit easier to breathe.

At the time, every single part of my body, heart, and brain was in pain. I remember feeling that I would have traded any physical pain that I had ever experienced in my life to be out of the misery and pain that I was in. I remember thinking that losing a limb would be less painful. I had never been a serious burn patient, but I would have preferred that, because I knew that I could come back from that. I knew that, as horrible as it was, I could heal from the burns. But how would I ever heal from this? Nothing was going to bring him back. There was nothing I could do to change that. Again, how would I ever come back from this? And if a person doesn't believe they will feel better, why endure? Why go on?

This is why a lack of hope is so dangerous with depression. This is why we can't really judge a person who has lost their life to suicide. They had been operating on a level of pain that was already unbearable, and everything in their mind had been telling them that it would not get better. This was the state they would exist in forever. They couldn't see the faulty thinking in that.

People would actually tell me in those days to be happier. They would say things like, "Joshua doesn't want you to be sad.". Or, they would say, "Don't stay sad forever.". Those words were asking me to do something I was incapable of doing. I often still am, but the light is getting brighter. I do have good days now. And I know that if I wait a little longer those days will be more frequent. To those experiencing depression... maybe asking you to believe it will get better is asking too much today. But I would challenge you to be scientific. Make a milepost to get to. Focus on that, and when you get there, pick another one. This is what you need to do to keep going. As you do this, you will find that each milepost gives another opportunity for something to get a bit easier. Be sure to invite someone along. Tell them your plan to get to the next milepost, or ask them to help you make that plan. What do you need to hobble along until you can walk? What do you need to walk, until you will be able to run later?

The other purpose of journaling or tracking is not only to help with milepost setting and being able to view progress, but it helps tremendously in diagnosing and getting the right treatment. I knew a friend who once a month would suffer from the worst depression. Her mood would just plummet, and she became extremely irritable to the people around her for several days. As I got to know her, I started to see a pattern. I asked her if it was the same time of the month every time. The light went on for her. She had not been able to put that together on her own. She suffered from PMDD (Premenstrual Dysphoric Disorder), which is a severe form of PMS, that has to do with irregular hormone changes. It would blindside her every month. Once she figured it out, she was able to talk to her doctor and get a plan together. It also helped that when it would set on again, she had a plan to cope.

If you can figure out your pattern those days might still be hard, but it is now in your head that it will not last. You can start to take precautions. Don't interview for a job during that time, or meet a new group of people. Do some self-care, so you don't cause damage to relationships during that episode, and you can get back to your normal routine quicker. Unfortunately, when a pattern is unclear, we make decisions in these depressive or mood disorder states that can cost us, in productivity and relationships. We are in danger of entering into a pattern of self-anger and negative self-talk. "I am a jerk." It seems very real and really hard to combat because, yes, in fact, you were a jerk. You said some things and you did some things that you regret now. But the difference in knowing, is that you can prevent it from happening in the future, and now you understand why it happened. You didn't decide to have mood swings that were out of control. You didn't decide to be so depressed that you couldn't go to the movies with your kid like you promised. You do care about people and want to be a good person in their lives. Now you can do better because you recognize when you need to step back and take care of yourself, so that, when you are present, you are the best version of yourself.

Can you see how this change in managing symptoms, and understanding patterns can prevent worsening symptoms, and self-hatred? This type of self-care makes all of the difference.

Make self-care a priority

This is a principal athletes use to optimize their performance. They will schedule rest days to give their muscles and bones a break from grueling, intense workouts. This is not merely a means for taking breaks. Often rest days for a runner involve yoga, walking, or some other type of active rest. But the body isn't actually taking a break. It's using the rest time to repair any damage that was done and to prepare itself to do better the next workout. The process of tearing down and building up of muscle is very important in transforming the body, and in the long run creates stronger and better performance.

This same concept can be applied to mental health. If you expect to run the same mental distance every day, you will burn out and not meet your goals. When you're in an episode of depression, it isn't a time to necessarily stay in bed, though you may. It's a time of active rest. For a client with chronic depression, I will encourage them to be aware of any suicidal thoughts and to engage in their safety plan. But I will also ask them to pull out the coping skills they have been learning and to actively use them. How is their inner dialogue? Is it unhelpful? Are they able to combat it on their own, or, do they need to call in their support system?

I cannot tell you how helpful it is to be around a person that I trust when I am struggling. I am very introverted and can still recognize how important this is. I usually don't even want to talk about what is wrong. I just need to know that I am not alone. And being around people helps me to maintain some clarity of thought. This active rest is a time to focus primarily on sleep and eating. It is easy to neglect those basic things when you brain is doing a lot of heavy lifting. But neglecting it can prolong the depressive episode. This active rest is a time to assess the basics, ask for extra help, and work to lessen negative self-talk. You are doing everything you need to do to smooth out the episode, reducing intensity, and duration.

For those supporting a loved one going through this, recognize that this isn't the day or week that they are going to accomplish some big goal they have set. Remind them that those goals will still be there in a few days. Or encourage them to break it up into smaller pieces and do one thing. And then don't let them beat themselves up for not doing more. You don't want to lose a race before you even get started.

Teach that suicide is an unacceptable choice

This topic is self-explanatory in principle and difficult in achieving. This should not be done in a condemning sort of way. You don't want to tell a person that they are broken because they have those thoughts or feelings. You want them to be able to talk about and express those things. You want them to know that no matter what, they need to try all of the options before suicide becomes a tempting option. Tell them," Let's try a, b, c, d, etc., Let's focus on that. I know you feel that life is painful and it is. It really is. But what if it won't be? Let's experiment. Let's just see.". And you walk that path with them. You are there with them when the first medication does not work, and they believe no medication will ever work. And you encourage them with, "There are other ones. This doesn't mean it is untreatable. Let's do a couple more steps."

Know your limits. Know that even if it isn't enough, you are enough

You cannot save a person from cancer, and you can't save them from depression. You can't. You do not have that control. You never had that control. Tell yourself that no matter how many times it takes to sink in. **<u>You cannot control whether a person dies or not.</u>** You are not omnipotent.

You can walk with them. You can encourage, and love, and teach them. Just as you can hold your loved one while they battle cancer, but you can't remove that disease, and you cannot treat it. But you can advocate that the best professionals are competently helping your loved one.

There's something I need to tell people in the mental health profession. You cannot take this illness away from those that you love any more than anyone else can take it from their loved ones. You cannot diagnose. You are too close. They are not your client or patient. Do not rely on a sense of thinking you have everything you need to help your loved one with this in your home. You wouldn't treat your loved one for cancer in your home either, even if you were an oncologist. Have someone else screen them.

Make a safety plan and contract

This is something to do with your loved one who is struggling along with their other trusted supports. It can also be done with a mental health professional, especially if a person has already survived an incomplete suicide. I have worked with chronic clients to develop a safety plan for certain events or times of the year that are especially difficult. This plan is individualized, takes into consideration chosen methods of suicide, and incorporates supports and coping skills. The plan is prescribed and is made a priority which can be adjusted as needed.

When we lost Joshua, I knew I needed to make a plan of recovery. I immediately asked the doctor to increase the medication I had been taking to address some mild depressive symptoms related to my diagnosis of PCOS. I also knew I would need at least a year of therapy. I knew I needed to reach out to supports. I needed medication to be able to sleep, and I needed to eat enough. I did not FEEL like doing any of those things. But I had an agreement with myself. I would do those things, and then reevaluate at a later point in time. I had to choose to do the things to keep me going for my girls, and I knew eventually I would need to find a reason for myself, but that is what I could cling onto at the time.

I also suffered from trauma triggers. Things would make my mind replay that night and I honestly couldn't think of anything else when that happened. So, I rearranged my house furniture. I replaced my front door, and bought new Christmas decorations, to reduce those associations. I was honest with medical professionals about suicidal ideations and other symptoms even when I felt like a failure. How dare I feel this way, when I know that it could hurt my family? I knew the pain this would cause. I had just been on the receiving end of it.

But that doesn't change how you feel. It just makes you feel worse that you feel that way. I had no faith that any of it would make a difference, even though I had sat with many individuals who had been through the worst of things, and they healed. But I decided to do all the things I KNEW would work, even when I didn't FEEL like they would work. And what I experienced was an up and down, two steps forward one step back type of recovery, with overall steady progress toward decreased symptoms.

As a point of comparison, my husband, while devastated by the loss of his son, did not experience suicidal ideation, and was able to work with a counselor for far less time to work through the feelings of grief and guilt. He didn't have to treat PTSD symptoms either. He got to a point of feeling remorse and regret that things happened the way they did, without holding on to a lot of the burden of blame. When a suicide occurs, everyone connected to that person will have to face two very daunting things. One, is the grief associated with losing that person. That never really ends. You will always miss that person, even if you learn to not have them around. You will always know that your life could have been better with them still in it. The other thing that has to be faced is the trauma of this type of loss. But we do know that there are tools to help with this. We just need to reach out for them and to have the courage to use them.

Look forward

Always have something that is scheduled and, on the calendar, to look forward to. I remember when I told my son that we decided not to go back to Utah for his grandparent's 50th Anniversary. With COVID, no one was able to gather and those that would, would be high risk. I remember hearing the disappointment in his voice. He had been working on a waltz for a present to give them. He was sweet like that. He also wrote a song for Mother's Day for me that same year.

So many things were cancelled that year because of COVID-19, and our youth took the biggest hit from it.

There is a lot of value in having something to look forward to. It gives you a reason to get up in the morning, to stay a little longer. It doesn't always have to be a trip to Disneyland, but anything really that someone likes to do. Ask your loved one what they look forward to. Support doesn't always have to be sitting with someone in their worst moments, but also taking time out of your life to have great moments. And that is what we are all fighting for. Life. Not survival. Life.

For those struggling, know that one day you will wake up and you will not be disappointed. One day, the sun will seem brighter and your mind clearer. Your body will be lighter and the ache will be gone. It will happen. Look forward to it, if you can.

I have been on both sides of that dark place, and, the morning after is glorious! Hang in there with me, with everyone around you. Your pain is something others feel, but you leaving will not erase it. It will make some of it permanent for them. Help them, and let them help you. Your life is precious and the pain is treatable. It hurts everyone, and only together can we all have the best, and happiest lives.

You are not alone. You matter. You are needed. You are loved.

Joshua's journal

A quick disclaimer: If you are currently struggling with suicidal ideation, reading this next part is potentially harmful at this time. Consider skipping it for now. To others, it takes another level of bravery and vulnerability for my family and I to share this. Joshua means everything to me. In his journals you will see the symptoms of depression and distorted thought processes. While it is difficult to share, I feel it has value in helping people to understand that though Joshua was experiencing all of the symptoms, he was not exhibiting behaviors to indicate these things. This is a very dangerous disorder. Joshua genuinely cared for people. If it could help one person to know that they aren't alone and to convince them to reach out and ask for help earlier than later, I believe he would want us to have the courage to share it.

April 9, 2018
What's up inanimate object known as paper? Today's episode of "Joshua Burgess's road to success" is brought to you by paper and the BIC mechanical pencil.

Aside from my fantastic entrance I have a life to narrate. If you noticed from previous discussion I'm planning to become a millionaire cellist. But that's a road paved with diamonds compacted by planning, practicing, and motivation. So I've hatched the first part of the plan. When we move to Nebraska I plan to open a YouTube channel and start throwing some music to people's ears. It can't be that hard can it. I mean, Joe posts videos about his day to day life and sometimes it's kind of fun to watch him do dares but that's as good as it gets and he has already made 7 cents.

JOSHUA'S JOURNAL

<u>April 18, 2018</u>
Whew, back to today. You see today is a special day for myself as it is the talent show tryouts and I smoked it! There were sixteen participants and I was able to play my whole song (Piano Guys "Cello Ascends")
I'm checking tomorrow for the second tryout, because I need to shorten the song. I just thinks its funny that I can perform a 3 minute song to a bunch of relative strangers, but I can't talk to T.

<u>April 21, 2018</u>
Cool things or people in life (not in order)
Simon and Garfunkl (I am a Rock)
Credence Clearwater Revival (Cotton field of Gold)
Cars (My Best Friend's Girl)
Franki Valli (Walk Like a Man)
Backman-Turner Overdrive (Takin care of Business)
All my good friends – Zach R., Seth G., Joe S., Aiden B. Ethan B. Kayson A., etc. (many more friends who can be listed later)
My favorite teachers = Mr. Loescher (Band), Mr. Clark (Geography), Mr. Bauer (Math) Mr. Peterson (Math) Mrs. Vasauckas (language arts) MRs. Mckee (Geography) Mrs. Gist (1st grade) Mr. Garcia (3rd grade)
All my fans = almost everyone.
Young women I would ask out if I was here longer – Teagan, Aubrie, Gracie, Shelby, etc.
My friend and cello = Roberto
Semi-automatic pump action 12 guage shotgun.
Imagine Dragons (warriors)
Toilet paper forts (Fred Meyers)

<u>April 22, 2018</u>
Aaaaay, yo what's up? Right now life is pretty awesome so I thought I's just right about it. Just yesterday, Zach, Aiden, Toby, and myself went to the Fred Meyers and built an awesome toilet paper fort with about three hundred dollars worth of rugs. Whenever someone passed by we'd make fart noises and they were so oblivious! After some time someone ratted us out to the manager and we'd have to put

back the rugs, but most of all the manager told us we had to leave and not come back for the rest of the day or in short terms we were temporarily kicked out. Afterwards we had a toast for our TP fort with some Martenelli Cider I bought. But, yeah. I had a pretty flippin good weekend. Sadly tomorrow I have to get up at 6:30 to go to school. Don't get me wrong, school's great. But honestly people, it's just not worth getting up at 6:30 in the morning and sitting for 5 and a half hours every day for almost all of the year. Anyways, like I said, I have to get up early so peace out.

April 25, 2018

Hello, I'm writing in my journal again because I'm bored and I just got told by my parents that my cello practice sounded bad enough to tell me to stop. But other than that I have some rather good news. Just yesterday we had a track meet that was particularly miserable due to the climate, rain/hail. However I did pretty well considering the weather, and the fact that I forgot my waterbottle. But that's not the good news. That nothin compared to the real victory, no, not at all. The good news is that I was able to talk to T at the meet: "Good luck, " "Go T" and "nice job" I was feelin pretty great about myself. I was like, "Oh yeah, I am the man, just said sic words to the hottest girl I know today!" So yes I felt great until Seth walks over saying, "yeah....that last time you talked, you had snot on your face." Now that, that was a good day!

Sep 23, 2018

Once again, I have procrastinated for 5 months. Man! I don't know where to start. I think I'll start on the last day of 7th grade. (two weeks before I moved to Nebraska.) That day was a blast! There was a huge party all over the campus. I got a genuine yearbook, and a lot of signatures from my friend, Some of the ladies, and even T. ☐ First I just wanna say I really miss my friends. My friends weren't the stereotypical [miscreant weak noodle] sittin in the back of the bus, making life appear as a horrible algebraic equation, meant to be manipulated and twisted until you find out that = sinning for Satan's own wicked amusement. No, my friends were the kind of people who showed me how to have a good time in a place that needs some ragtag hooligan teenagers to spice things up with an elevator, a few dodge balls, some toilet paper, Or perhaps just talking to a cute girl. My point is: If you have good friends, you will remember each one and you will remember how they each took part in the better things that make you.

October 4, 2018

Today was a wash: I went to school, signed up for a club that's for helping "special" kids, had some laughs with my friends, ran four miles and went home. But the reason that makes today sick tis the fact that my new MP3 player might be broken. I loved that thing like a brother! It was one of the greatest friends, that I carried to school every day and listened to the Beatles any time I could! And yet after a matter of weeks it might be dead.

It's just that there are so many things to do and remember. Music is a break from all that. And I can carry it in my pocket!....Unless for some reason, My MP3 player breaks.

October 7, 2018

Just writin to say everythings fine now and the MP3 player's okey.

Today's Sunday on Conference weekend. The prophets mostly talked about ministering and stuff like that. I'm not entirely sure why but I feel inspired to invite this kid named Michael to church. No Michael is probably in need of the gospel more than others in his daily life. The reason being for the assumption would be that he told me about his depression and suicide attempt.

Some days Michael seems like an okay guy, others I can't tell whether or not he considers me a friend or foe. Bad days are clear as mud and yet just as obvious.

I haven't seen a good day for Michael in a while and I'm startin to get worn out by his displays of hopelessness.

On another note; Just the other day, I went to my first stake dance. It was pretty fun. It lasted for about four hours and I danced with three girls. One of them asked me to dance, but that's okay because I asked Cally, and Cadence.

The DJ was taking requests and I got them to play "Hey Jude" and "The Rainbow Connection".

October 20, 2018

Ya know, I feel pretty good right now. I feel ready to go do something important regardless of what others might frown upon.

I feel that all is well with the world even though reality says otherwise.

And I know that someday I will do something important and that one day, all will be well with the world.

In a world full of distractions, it can be hard to remember just how blessed we are. It can be hard to make small sacrifices to help others less fortunate than you or I. And it's even harder to hear and know what to do.

January 4, 2019

Well it's been awhile and a lot of things have happened. First of all I've been catching up with my friend Ethan for the past week. Ethan is probably the best friend I will ever have. I've known him since I was seven and until now I haven't seen him for six years except for two or three visits. Over the years Ethan has endured struggles that I cannot imagine.

For Ethan's sake I will not record them. And in the same but seemingly different way, I have undergone trials and horribly failed at times, but as the band Styx once said, "So if you think your life is complete confusion because you never win the game, just remember that it's a grand illusion and deep inside we're all the same."

To me this sheds light on the fact that, even if life seems particularly crappy for you, it's all been done before and everyone struggles whether you know it or not. And when I think about the Grand – Illusion I remember that life is not about who has the brightest light-up sneakers or the thicker wallet, life is about the choices we make, the things we do, the promises we keep and the things we learn.

January 22, 2019

Hey, how's life treatin you. Just yesterday I heard that my friend was in the hospital. It pisses me off that I'm not there to help my friend.

For the past while I've really felt sorrow over the fact that my greatest friend lives in Nevada where he endures great illness, all the friends I've made over the past five years all live in Alaska (to include T) and then a girl I really care for (whom I've known for almost as long as Ethan) has moved from Hawaii to Maryland. But I live in Nebraska.

Here in Nebraska I don't have any friends that I can talk to. Girls seem distant and I intend to fix that somehow.

Another thing is that Mom and Dad think I'm gonna work in a cubicle or something. But that is not the case. Someday Roberto and I are gonna hit it big.

So, life's changing and I guess I don't know what to made of it. I don't know whether its good or bad. I guess I'll call it good and make sure that's how things turn out from time to time. Just the other day I found out there's another girl here named T so I figured I'd try to get her number. However I was to wimpy to ask for her number, so I gave her mine and got out of there real quick. So far she hasn't texted me yet and I don't know if I should be dismayed yet.

<u>March 13, 2019</u>

Yo, Howdy.

It's been a little bit, but a lots happened since I last wrote. Five days ago was my first quad stake dance and lets just say, I came in swingin and ended up knockin quite a few out of the park. Though, most of them I don't remember many of them.

I mainly just remember dancing with K (from school), E (because my friends told me to), and M (she's from my ward, she's my friends older sister and my mom thinks she's too old, but she's just two years ahead of me.) The Wednesday before the quad stake dance, a girl I kinda like caught me off guard, as I passed her heading out the door, when she said, "Hey Josh, you're gorgeous!" And she was all smiley like. So I was just like "Uh……thanks." And just split outa there like a banana. Anyways when the dance came I was going to try to dance with her but I waited to long and she went home sick. Also, I started a thing with Merrick, myself and Cameron by jumping in circles around the gym.

<u>April 4, 2019</u>

Right now at this moment, I am in love with my life and my life is treatin' me good! I feel as though I don't need any material posessions at this moment. I could be the greatest musician of all time. I could be the raddest kid on the block. I could party with my friends and family in heaven and on Earth. And best of all I actually can do all of those.

In writing all of that, I was not on drugs but rather listening to some good tunes.

<u>On Earth, I have some goals, the first of them is to carry my family line down, and the second is to make people feel spiritual emotions upon hearing my music.</u>

June 2, 2019

I'm disappointed, confused, stressed, annoyed, pissed, brought down, a little lonely, and most of all I'm fearing like I could possibly be deserving less. That's all for today.

February 14, 2020

Today's Valentine's Day, but I don't really care. Lately I've realized I really like someone but I don't think they feel the same. I do my best to smile but it tears me up inside. Another thing I've realized is that some people aren't with me till I'm on the ground; and it's because of this that I can't trust anybody with my thoughts. For example; you wouldn't have somebody spot you on the bench if they didn't pay attention until you were half crushed.

These things that I talk about....they knock me down. But if I'm gonna go down, I'm gonna go down for something worth purpose. I'm honestly afraid of being meaningless and I hate letting people down. I can't trust anybody who doesn't trust me and I can't give what I don't have.

July 29, 2020

It's been weird lately; I've been talking to M a lot lately. I figure she likes me, namely because I told her I like (still do) and she said she likes me too. (geez, my handwriting is so bad) But, a lot more than that has happened and a lot more is happening. Corona virus is still very much present right now and we're starting school in about two weeks. After a lot of discussion and stress my parents decided to let me go to school (physically). I'm not worried about getting sick. If I do, the worst thing that could happen is that I wouldn't be able to play football. I'm not playing this year because my parents are scared. My parents don't like me much. I don't doubt that they care about me. They just don't trust me to be a good person. I don't blame them. I don't trust myself to be a good person. I also kinda don't like myself. I'm too small. I'm to weak. I'm to needy and I'm too insecure.....it's been weird lately.

September 18, 2020

I'm supposed to be sleeping right now. But, I had a thought that I needed to record. I read somewhere that the good things in life happen after a lot of time and effort, but the best things in life just happen.

I have decided this is true for me. In the mortal life we plan and work hard for what we think is a good life, but, if we live according to

God's plan, that's when our lives are blessed beyond anything imaginable.

The main message is that we must understand that God intends for us to be happy and joyous. Though we might not know it at the time. I didn't decide to have the amazingly wonderful friends I have now. God did, and I'm so thankful for that. Goodnight!

October 14, 2020

I lost a friend a few weeks ago and it was my fault. I'm not going to clarify much more than that. We're still kinda friends right now but a lot of things are changing right now and I'm exhausted.

I don't really enjoy life anymore. The only reason I wake up in the morning is because I know that sometimes we have to do hard things and I like a challenge. I don't know how many L's I can take. It's hard for me to uphold gospel standards and Christ-like mindsets when it's so much more attainable to be a "bad person". I hope I don't go to hell. Maybe, I will try to get some numbers from some cute girls. Either way, I will keep fighting for now.

October 15, 2020

Everywhere I go, I have to prove to people that I belong there by acting a certain way or doing something. I feel safest in the weight room but I know I'm judged and have always been judged because I'm small and skinny. Somehow, I feel safest in the weight room because it's the only place I don't need somebody to tell me I belong there. I go there because I know I belong there and someday, if I don't kill myself before then, I'll prove to everyone else that the weight room is my room.

I'm not sure if I should keep trying to be a genuine good person who tries to be better everyday, or be a bad person who doesn't care about things outside of his world, or if I should just die. I know the first option is the "best" option, but I wake up contemplating whether or not it's worth it to be alive every morning. I still haven't gotten an answer. I have a testimony of the gospel and I know that it's teachings are true. I just don't have faith in myself and I'm very tired.

11/15/2020
Sunday

Joshua Burgess

To all those it may concern,

    For those of you who have forgotten me, my name is Joshua Burgess. I have three little sisters and a loving mother and father. We are a spunky family and I love everyone in my family. Anna (the oldest) is a fighter and I'm so proud of how she has coped with her trials. Nadya (the middle) is so compassionate and I hope she finds a way to live life continually growing stronger and understanding. Sarah (the youngest) is a dreamer and she's the happiest little girl who wants to be a marine biologist when she grows up. I know that she will achieve her dreams even if they change. My mother is the strongest person I know. My mom has so many burdens she carries with her all the time and while she loses patience sometimes, she gets so many things done on a regular basis it's inhuman. She has suffered infirmities mental and physical and still she fights for us everyday. My father is my role model. My dad doesn't know it, but he taught me how to laugh and how I should take care of the people I love. I've always wanted to be like my dad but I found out that it's a lot harder to laugh than I thought and it's impossible for me to take care of the people I love.

    I don't know if anybody cares enough to read about me but I'm going to write about myself anyways. I don't know how long I was depressed but I've been suicidal for at least two months. I try to fight always but everyday is the same fight as the last and I don't know who's winning anymore. I wake up at 5 am every morning and it's so much harder when I wish I didn't have to wake up at all. See back →

JOSHUA'S JOURNAL

11/20/2020

I am not your stereotypical teenage suicide that doesn't believe they have accomplished anything. I truly believe that if it wasn't for my night shift, I would have gave in to amazing things. I've always had big dreams. I wanted to end up famous, not for the glory of it, but to inspire and uplift the broken hearted like me. I've always looked to iconic athletes for inspiration and motivation to live life everyday. I wanted to be famous for overcoming odds that no one believed I could, so that kids would see that someone as skinny as them can grow to be strong even when everyone else believes. I wanted to have influence like Tyler Holland so that kids would see that even someone with depression can write beautiful lyrics that strengthen God's children. I wanted to prove to them that even though they feel so alone, that they are truly loved by someone.

To me, one of the most beautiful things in life is when someone is broken down and they only rise higher. I've had the blessing to experience this as God has given me trials in my life. No one would have guessed that I would be as physically strong as I am now, but with God's wisdom I became this way. But in my weakness, I have decided to give up on a particular trial. While I can accomplish great things on my own, when I try to be around people I love, I only bring them down and make them sadder. I'm too broken and selfish to care for anyone.

11/21/2020

These are my final words and thoughts for the world. The American Revolution was the shot heard around the world. I guess I'm just wondering who will hear my shot. I'm disgusted with my self centered-ness, even in death. I fail in this last step. My trials but you put a worthier burden than for any other life. I'm grateful for the life I had and the love I was able to know for a little while. Lastly, I am sorry to anyone I hurt in life. I hope I don't hurt you in death.

Joshua's Note:
15 Nov 2020

For those of you who have forgotten me, my name is Joshua Burgess. I have three little sisters and a loving mother and father. We are a spunky family and I love everyone in my family. Anna (the oldest) is a fighter and I'm so proud of how she has coped with her trials. Nadya (the middle) is so compassionate and I hope she finds a way to live life continually growing stronger and understanding. Sarah (the youngest) is a dreamer and she's the happiest little girl who wants to be a marine biologist when she grows up. I know that she will achieve her dreams even if they change. My mother is the strongest person I know. My mom has so many burdens she carries with her all the time and while she loses patience sometimes, she gets so many things done on a regular basis it's inhuman. She has suffered infirmities mental and physical and still she fights for us every day. My Father is my role model. My dad doesn't know it, but he taught me how to laugh and how I should take care of the people I love. I've always wanted to be like my dad but I found out that it's a lot harder to laugh than I thought and it's impossible for me to take care of the people I love.

I don't know if anybody cares enough to read about me but I'm going to write about myself anyway. I don't know how long I've been depressed but I've been suicidal for at least two months. I love to fight adversary but every day is the same fight as the last and I don't know who's winning anymore. I wake up at 5 am every morning and it's so much harder when I wish I didn't have to wake up at all. See Back →

20 Nov 2020

I am not your stereotypical teenage suicide that doesn't believe they have accomplished anything. I firmly believe that if it weren't for my mental state, I would have gone on to do amazing things. I've always had big dreams. I wanted to end up famous, not for the glory of men, but to inspire and uplift the broken hearted like me. I've always looked to iconic athletes for inspiration and motivation to live life every day. I wanted to be famous for overcoming odds that no one believed I could, so that kids would see that someone as skinny as them can grow to be strong even when no one else believes. I wanted to have influence like Elder Holland so that kids would see that even someone with depression can write beautiful talks that strengthen God's children. I wanted to prove to them that even though they feel so alone, that they are truly loved by someone.

To me, one of the most beautiful things in life is when someone is beaten down and they only rise higher and I've had the blessing to experience this as God has given me trials in my life. No one would have guessed that I would be as physically strong as I am now, but with God's blessing I have become this way. But in my weakness, I have decided to give up on a particular trial. While I can accomplish great things on my own, when I try to be around people I love I only bring them down and make them sad. I'm too broken and selfish to care for anyone.

21 Nov 2020

These are my final words and thoughts for the world. The American Revolution was the shot heard around the world, so I guess I'm just wondering who will hear my shot. I'm disgusted with how self-centered I am, even in death I fail to think of others. My trials hurt me but I wouldn't trade them for any other life. I'm grateful for the life I had and the love I was able to know for a short little while. Lastly, I am sorry to anyone I hurt in life. I hope I don't hurt you in death.

The Afterward ;

I think a lot about those first few days after Joshua passed. I was so nauseous, and even with medication, I couldn't sleep. We moved the girls' mattresses into our room. I couldn't bear to have them separated from me. There was no way I could sleep without knowing for sure they were safe. I remember the first time one of my daughters walked outside at night afterward, and how my heart stopped. She was just going to the next-door neighbor to deliver something. We didn't have many answers in the beginning. When a death like this occurs, an investigation takes place and you aren't told very much. We didn't get his suicide note or his phone till many weeks after. It was a strange thing to have the investigator talk to us that night. He asked us if we had plans for a burial or cremation. A few hours before I didn't even know my son had died. Later the investigator also told us that Joshua's death was out of the ordinary from the others he had seen. His note wasn't a quick, short message of goodbye. He had started writing about himself a week before he passed, and finished it the night he died. I hate that I am grateful for that note. But Joshua answered some of the questions that most families don't get answered. And I do believe the things he wrote can help many others. That note is included in the previous chapter of this book.

The trauma triggers from the night my son passed became so significant for me that every night we had to make sure that all of the windows were covered. We replaced our front door because every time I passed it, I would think of that night and how he never came back through it. I could not read or concentrate on anything for months afterwards and though the days were difficult, the evenings were even worse because of the triggering memories, and also because that was the

THE AFTERWARD ;

time we spent together as a family. Weekends were hard for the same reason. I hated waking up in the morning. It felt like a brutal assault to have the knowledge he was gone force itself into my consciousness. There is relief when you wake from a nightmare. But I would wake up to a nightmare. My husband would put calming music on in the morning to help.

There are so many hard things with a loss like this. It was hard when a week after he died, college recruitment letters started showing up along with condolence cards. I was still getting emails from the college board about ways to prepare my student for college. I forgot to let his driver's ed teacher know that he had passed and a few days after his passing we came home and she was waiting in front of our house for his last scheduled practice drive.

I had to learn to answer questions like, "How many children do you have?", or "So, you only have girls?"

Seeing updates about his friends was both hard and helpful. I wanted to see them living life. I wanted to know that they were going to be ok, but I also wanted my son to be in their pictures and in the stories that they were still making.

I couldn't feel gratitude very easily in those beginning days. That emotion was beyond me. There was not a lot of room for anything beyond pain and sorrow.

However, it seemed every day, there was someone there to support us in some way. There were meals, cards, meaningful gifts, and tearful hugs. Our community mourned our son with us.

A couple of days after Joshua passed, a meeting was arranged for the youth in the community. It was a chance for them to meet with therapists and to process this loss together. My husband, oldest daughter, and I attended, and my husband and I expressed to the youth that this was not their fault. From the moment I found out about Joshua, I had a great anxiety for his friends. I was so worried for them and I knew that Joshua would not want them to blame themselves. He often expressed his concern and care for his friends to me, and I knew he would want us to tell them to try to not carry guilt with them. The youth wrote things about Joshua and we were gifted a book with their thoughts and memories.

We ended up having two funerals, one in Nebraska, and one in Utah. This was because the majority of our family lives in Utah. The funeral in Nebraska was open to the public, and attended by many students from

THE AFTERWARD ;

his school, along with administrators, and teachers. People from Jon's work and mine attended to support, along with people from our church and other friends.

I remember that a couple of Joshua's friends hugged me at the funeral, and they were taller than me, and it was a comfort to me because it felt so similar to when I would hug my son.

Jon's work friends donated money for our family to be able to do some things on a trip we had planned for the week after Joshua died. It was a trip nearby that had been planned several months before. We debated about whether it was best to go, but ultimately decided we would benefit from getting away from the house.

Joshua was a member of the Intergenerational Orchestra in Omaha, along with his cello, 'Roberto'. Orchestra members donated money to help with funeral arrangements. There were so many gifts and kind thoughts given. I had a new friend who took me to lunch and just let me talk and cry. Another friend held my hand during a particularly difficult day and just sobbed with me. My sister called regularly to check on me, let me talk when I needed, and gave me space when I couldn't do anything but exist.

When we got back from the funeral in Utah, we pulled up into the driveway after dark, but there were Christmas lights hung outside with other decorations. This was done by our friends from church mostly, but our neighbors assisted as well. I couldn't tell them that I had been dreading coming home because the memories would be even stronger. That was such a special gift. It made it possible to get out of the car and go inside the house. The joy in my girls' voices was a balm to me. When we got in the house, the living room was full of Christmas gifts. It looked like Christmas and Santa had already come. There was fresh fruit and milk in the house, purchased by a friend, and the house had been cleaned by the ladies from church. Anna's room was covered in decorations, and birthday gifts. She had turned 14 while we were in Utah and her friends wanted her to feel loved and special.

A while before Joshua passed, he had started composing a waltz for his grandparents 50th anniversary which was on De. 19th. We didn't think that we would be able to make it to the anniversary as we would have to travel to Utah and most people wouldn't be able to attend because of covid. When I told Joshua he was so disappointed. I told him maybe we could do a visit between Christmas and the New Year. He had been working on that project and had left several recordings of his

THE AFTERWARD ;

progress as he was creating. We ended up at his grandparents without him on their 50th anniversary. It was a somber celebration. Only Jon, I, and the girls knew of the project at the time. A little while later I found a talented friend who had also lost a nephew to suicide around the same time as Joshua, and she wrote music as well. She generously offered to finish the project for us. There will be so many things that feel unfinished, and things we will miss out of with Joshua, and this was a precious gift for us. You can find that song by looking for Valerie Olson and Joshua Burgess – Joshua's Waltz or by using the QR code.

There were so many special things that people did for us in those months. I cannot express how special each call, text message, tear shed on our behalf, prayer spoken for us, and everything else was. There wasn't anything anyone could do to remedy our sorrow, but I and my family were carried in our grief.

I had someone say about 10 months afterwards, "I don't know how you are doing it?" I just thought to myself, medication and therapy certainly help. The reality was that I wasn't doing it on my own. I know my limits of strength. When you struggle with low energy levels, you are always aware of your limits. And I know that my limits were surpassed every day, and each day someone had been there to help me in both small, and huge ways. Each day is a different challenge, and what I needed the day after it happened, and what I need now is different.

When this trauma changed my whole world and made me question everything that I thought I knew, I had to reevaluate and build a new life. I also had to build a new me, a me that would be able to survive and live in this new reality. There is a reason that those affected by this type of tragedy are called survivors of suicide loss. There were more questions than answers right after Joshua passed, but the first thing that I had to reassure me, was the constant care of those around us. It reaffirmed to me that we are all connected through the same things. We all love and we all experience pain and sorrow. And we are not alone.

There are some answers we will never get. We cannot know if the disease was primarily genetically driven, or if it the medication that he had taken earlier that year was a catalyst. It could have been a combination of multiple things. When the comedian Robin Williams died, his family didn't have many answers either, though they knew that he had experienced depression, anxiety, paranoia, and impaired cognition. None of that was the smart, funny, and engaging actor that the world knew. It wasn't until after he passed that the extent of his brain disease was discovered. He suffered from a progressive Lewy body disease.

For those affected by suicide, the reason and the illness may be different, but the truth is that people do not die from suicide because they want to hurt people. Suicide is neither a reflection of who they are, the life they lived, or the people in their lives.

I cannot say that I am all the way through this. I am not really even certain what that would mean, but I can say that I can see a way forward now, when I couldn't in the beginning. There are still a lot of rough days, and I still cry most days at some point. But I am able to get up, and take care of my kids. I am able to work on projects, and have begun working again. I still attend therapy regularly, but it doesn't feel as vital as before. I deal with brain fog on the worst of days, but it isn't everyday anymore. I no longer have to close the blinds at night, and though difficult I was able to allow my kids to join their friends to go trick or treating at Halloween. I have hope for the future, and that, is beyond amazing.

My girls are making friends in our new community, and they are involved in activities. They are laughing easier, and they are looking forward to Christmas this year. They aren't the same, and they never will be. They will always carry some sorrow with them, and they will be more empathetic to others because of it. They can't stand to see siblings be unkind to each other, and they sometimes worry for their mom. When they caught me crying in the beginning, I could see the worry and even fear in their eyes. I think we all watched each other closely, treating each other as if we were fragile and could disappear. I don't cry as frequently anymore and when they catch me, they give me a hug and I don't see the fear. I believe that they have learned that you can keep going and really all that we can control is embracing each other when we can.

It has been a slow process to regain trust in those around me. The process requires me to learn to trust my children to make safe choices, and to trust myself to be able to parent well, and to have good judgement in different situations.

Someone told me that this experience will enlarge my capacity to be compassionate and understanding towards others. I feel it is much too high of a price, but I have found some peace in helping others. It calms the part of my heart that regrets not being able to do more for my son.

I don't know what specifically the future holds, but I know there will be challenges. There will be beautiful moments as well. For me, I will do my best to live each day, even when that means just surviving that day, to be here for the wonderful days. And I will continue to fight for a life of purpose and love, because those are the only things that matter.

After going through this, so many things seem so insignificant. Some of the things in life that we see as important don't mean as much as we might think. I regret many things, but I do not regret having Joshua for a son. I am a better person for knowing him, and loving him. We can never get everything right. It is impossible. But we can love people perfectly with some practice. It starts with loving ourselves, and then those around us. That is the bit we have some control of.

The following is the last text my husband sent to my son.

THE AFTERWARD ;

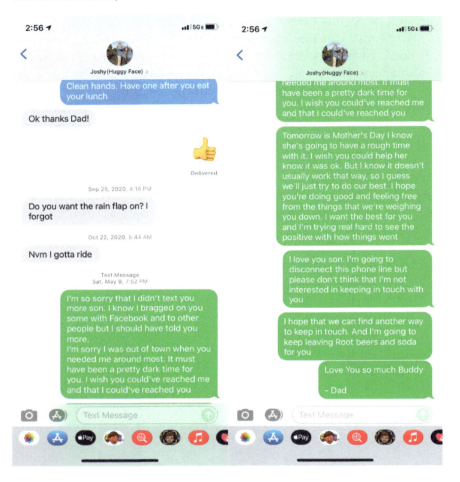

In the week leading up to Joshua's death, there were some tender moments that I had with him. One of those was in the evening, while I was playing the piano. I was playing "I See the Light" from Disney's *Tangled*. It had a sweet melody and was about seeing the light, and about seeing the world completely new. We can all relate to that. Sometimes we are in a fog until one day the fog dissipates, and the world is beautiful; life is beautiful. Joshua got his guitar out and said, "I can play along with you". He then started playing chords that beautifully blended with the piano. I cannot hear that song and not think of him. It's bittersweet. May we all have more light in our lives.

THE AFTERWARD ;

Joshua Christian Burgess - Obituary
September 4, 2004 – November 21, 2020

Joshua passed away unexpectedly from an unseen illness November 21, 2020. He is survived by his parents, Maria and Jonathan Burgess, his three younger sisters, Anna, Nadya, and Sarah; grandparents Lorna and Darvin Burgess, and Jeffery Chaston; and his many cousins, aunts, and uncles who are heartbroken with his passing. Joshua was a Sophomore at Papillion-LaVista South High school, where he was an honor student. Joshua was an athlete and musician; he played cello, piano, guitar, and some other instruments that he had begun to learn. He was a member of the Intergeneration Orchestra of Omaha and enjoyed music in all genres and generations. He was also a seminary student in the Church of Jesus Christ of Latter-Day Saints. He enjoyed telling jokes and writing music with his sisters, playing football, weightlifting, running, teasing his mom, being in the outdoors with his father, and spending time with his many friends who will miss him greatly.

He was compassionate, funny, intelligent, and strong. If we have learned anything from Joshua's passing it is that the best among us, the ones with the most promise and potential, with every advantage and happiness in this life, are not invincible to the tragic reaches of depression. Joshua will be missed more than words can describe, and while we have learned something from his death, we can learn much more from the life he lived in his short 16 years. He loved genuinely; he truly saw the people around him. He embraced life and new experiences. He was a faithful disciple of Christ who served diligently in his church and community and honored his parents. His family will miss him greatly and will hold on to the peace that comes from knowing that families are forever and will one day be together again.

Eulogy for Joshua, shared Dec. 4, 2020, and presented by Darvin Burgess (paternal grandfather). Written by Maria Burgess.

Joshua was born in the Monterey Bay area in California on September 9th, 2004. He then moved several times within Texas and California, until he moved to Alaska at the age of 9. He then moved to Nebraska at the

THE AFTERWARD ;

age of 13. In Joshua's life he visited 4 countries, and 34 states, several national parks, and all adjoining bodies of water to the Unites States, including the Gulf of Mexico, The Pacific, the Atlantic, and the Arctic Ocean. He had swum in the ocean in Hawaii, toured the halls of the White House, and eaten Muktuk in Alaska. He has seen Mt. Denali, and hiked in the German Alps, the Rockies, Sierras, Ozarks, and the Great Smokies. His favorite food was Clam chowder which he learned to love from visiting the Wharfs in California and would ask his mother to make that for several of his birthdays. He has friends in multiple states and continents at this time that mourn his passing with us. Though Joshua had traveled a lot, he was also grounded in familial roots. When asked to choose between various exciting destinations or traveling to Utah to see family, Joshua would vote Utah. He loved his Grandparents, cousins, and aunts and uncles.

Joshua ran his first official 5k with his mother in Utah on one of these trips, when he was 8. His last recorded PR for a mile was 5:30. His parents ran with him when he was young and didn't let him win a footrace, telling him soon they wouldn't be able to keep up with him and would need to take the victories as long as they could. Joshua ran with his mother this last month, patiently, as she struggled with injuries that prevented actual running speeds. Joshua enjoyed playing football as a freshman, and as a sophomore became very interested in weightlifting.

Joshua began to learn to play piano in 3rd grade, and developed a love-hate for it at first, sometimes complaining to his mom about the practice required. Per Burgess family policy, Joshua completed two years of piano before he could then select another instrument, and chose the cello, being inspired by the piano guys, Steven Nelson, and then other artists like Two Cellos. Joshua enjoyed combining classic instruments with modern music and would be heard playing groups like ACDC on his cello. He then decided to teach himself the guitar because according to him, 1. It is an instrument that is easier to pack and take with him, which he often did when camping with family, and parties with friends, and 2. Girls like guys who play the guitar. Joshua enjoyed spending time writing music with his sister, Anna, who would write the lyrics, while Joshua would give some input and write the music. The two of them had their first band, the Fire Griffins, with a neighbor friend in Alaska, when they were 6 and 9 and had their first gig playing for a local AM family station. Joshua shared his love of music by sharing songs or artists with friends and family and would create songs to give as a gift to family members.

THE AFTERWARD ;

Joshua's life was like the opening lines of a song, with an interesting chord progression, and the beginning of a melody fit for lyrics that feel like a story being told. We have been left with just enough to know it will be a masterpiece, because it sounds beautiful and exciting. Epic really. But we are jolted by the abrupt stop to that song.

For those that are unfamiliar with our faith, we believe there was a life in Heaven before this mortal existence where we counseled with our Father in Heaven and chose to come to this Earth to learn the things we would need to know, to progress toward becoming like our Father in Heaven. We believe in eternity. A difficult concept for a limited perspective of this life. Joshua did many things in his short sixteen years. More than many can claim themselves, but it is easy to think of the many milestones that he has yet to complete. In the context of our Faith, and in Joshua's faith, Joshua accomplished some of the most important things in this life and has taken those things with him.

He learned to love as the Savior does. We have heard numerous stories of Joshua doing little acts of service in quiet ways. In middle school, Joshua would fist bump his teachers almost daily. This was his way of saying "thank you." And "I value you even though you gave me an assignment I didn't like." He carried this to High School where he would take the time to tell his teachers to have a good day. Several times over the last few years, I can recall Joshua coming to us about friends who had confided in him about serious things that they had been struggling with. He expressed genuine love and concern. He was quick to offer an encouraging word to those around him. He served in his church as a Priest gladly and had been preparing to service a mission after graduating High school.

When setting goals this year, he set fitness goals, which of course does not surprise those that knew him. He also set a goal to spend more quality time with each of his sisters, Anna, Nadya, and Sarah. He would try to prioritize this time often enduring activities that were low on his preference list. He also set goals in his religious course this year which were to read his scriptures regularly and to come closer to his Heavenly Father. When we would read scriptures as a family, he would often tell us he had already read that bit. He understood the Atonement as a process of using repentance to follow in his Savior's steps and to receive comfort in his challenges. Last year, Joshua wrote this to a friend who was going through a very difficult time, "even though I don't entirely know the pains you endure, Christ has suffered them all. And if it ever seems like nobody understands what you're going through, he knows exactly what you're dealing with and knows what you need." He knew his Savior because he strived to walk in his footsteps. Perhaps this is also because he was shown a lot of love in his life. There wasn't a day of his life that he was not embraced or told that he was loved. We can see this by so many sorrowful hearts that he left behind. His many friends here today, and teachers, leaders, and military life-long friends, and those attending virtually.

    Even though we cannot hear the next part of his song, does not mean that it is not being written. Joshua is still the intelligent, funny, strong, creative, handsome young man, who is a loving son, brother, and Priesthood holder with strong faith. When the day comes, we look forward to hearing more of Joshua's song and have peace in knowing that families can be together forever. Until then we will work toward learning to love a little better, and to be kind as Joshua has shown us.

THE AFTERWARD ;

The following images are entries in a grief journal created by Joshua's youngest sister, Sarah, and are shared with her permission.

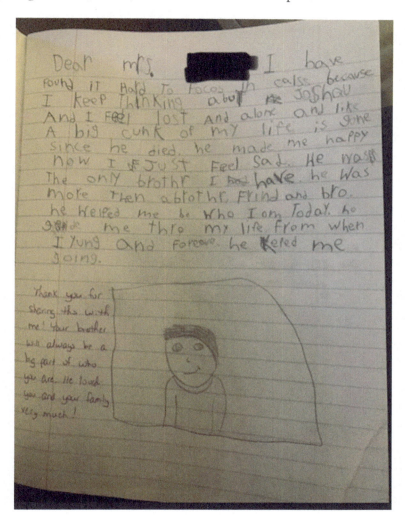

THE AFTERWARD ;

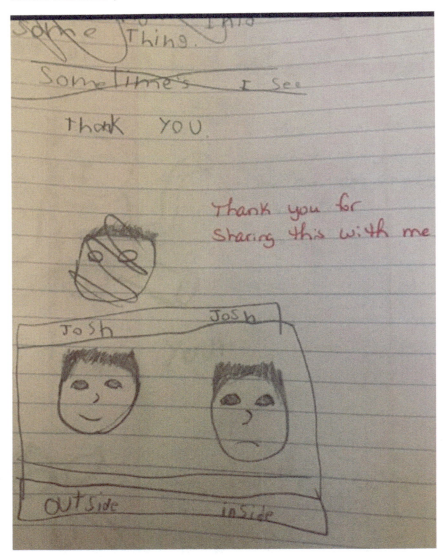

THE AFTERWARD ;

References and Resources

American Psychiatric Association. (2013). *Diagnostic and statistical manual of mental disorders* (5th ed.). Arlington, VA: Author.

 [Breaking point: How one Utah community is winning the fight against suicide - Deseret News](#)

Inoue K, Tanii H, Fukunaga T, Abe S, Nishimura Y, Kaiya H, Nata M, Okazaki Y. A correlation between increases in suicide rates and increases in male unemployment rates in Mie prefecture, Japan. Ind Health. 2007 Jan;45(1):177-80. doi: 10.2486/indhealth.45.177. PMID: 17284891.

Kennard, B. D., Silva, S. G., Tonev, S., Rohde, P., Hughes, J. L., Vitiello, B., Kratochvil, C. J., Curry, J. F., Emslie, G. J., Reinecke, M., & March, J. (2009). Remission and recovery in the Treatment for Adolescents with Depression Study (TADS): acute and long-term outcomes. *Journal of the American Academy of Child and Adolescent Psychiatry, 48*(2), 186–195. https://doi.org/10.1097/CHI.0b013e31819176f9

Morgan, E. (2014, April 26). *Breaking Point: How one Utah community is winning the fight against suicide.* Deseret News. https://www.deseret.com/2014/4/26/20540265/breaking-point-how-one-utah-community-is-winning-the-fight-against-suicide#jamie-nagle-former-mayor-of-syracuse-talks-about-the-decline-in-the-number-of-suicides-in-the-city-on-monday-april-21-2014

Russell R, Metraux D, Tohen M. Cultural influences on suicide in Japan. Psychiatry Clin Neurosci. 2017 Jan;71(1):2-5. doi: 10.1111/pcn.12428. Epub 2016 Sep 13. PMID: 27487762.

 [Depression, the secret we share | Andrew Solomon - Bing video](#)

 PET scan of the brain for depression - Mayo Clinic

 Drowning Rats Psychology Experiment: Resilience and the Power of Hope - The World of Work Project

 Home | NAMI: National Alliance on Mental Illness

 Home | AFSP

[Lifeline (suicidepreventionlifeline.org)](suicidepreventionlifeline.org)

Terminology of The Church of Jesus Christ of Latter-Day Saints

Bishop – the leader of a local congregation (known as a ward) with responsibilities similar to pastor, priest, or rabbi. In The Church of Jesus Christ of Latter-Day Saints, this position is unpaid.

Stake – A stake is a group of local Church congregations. A stake generally consists of about 3,000 to 5,000 members in five to ten congregations.

Stake President – A man who is asked to serve as a volunteer in this position. He oversees Church programs in a defined geographical area composed of individual congregations called wards (similar to a Catholic Diocese)

Acknowledgments

In the months after Joshua's death, the urge to share this message was uncomfortable, at times almost as much as the yearning that I have for my son, and I couldn't not share it. Each day has been difficult, and I can honestly say that I know the reason why I am not just surviving but learning to live again is because of the many friends and supportive loved ones in my life. I cannot thank everyone here adequately, but please know that every kind word of condolence or encouragement, every act of service, and well-thought gift added up to a sum of support that made not only getting through this difficult year possible, but also this book. What has felt impossible has become possible through the joint effort of many.

I want to express a special thanks to Jenn, Justin, Starla, Lorena, Desirae, and Dustin for your help in making this happen. Thank you for helping to make sure that the message is clear and for honoring my son by joining in this effort. To my daughters, Anna, Nadya, and Sarah, you are the light in my life and I am so proud of your courage, and your caring hearts. I know that you will grow into strong and beautiful women as you are already people that I look up to and you bring joy to everyone in your lives. To Joshua's friends, I want to say thank you for adding joy to Joshua's life, and to those that also have shared parts of their stories. Please continue to support one another and know that you are amazing just as you are. I think of you often.

To my husband, who has spent many hours reading and editing, grieving with me, and encouraging me to share this message when insecurity and doubt would have become barriers to completing it, I love you. I could not have chosen a better father for my children.

For Joshua, I miss you kiddo. Thank you for teaching those around you with your example of genuine friendship, for the meaningful conversations that have made me a better person, and for the joy and laughter you brought to my life. It was everything and yet not enough. I will carry you with me always.